JOHN WILSON was a firefi
He served in Belfast and acr
was Development Producer o
Firefighters on the Front Line,
He lives in Magheralin with his wife. This is his first
book.

Firefighters
during the
Troubles

The men and women
on the frontline tell
their stories

JOHN WILSON

·THE·
BLACK
·STAFF·
PRESS

First published in 2019 by Blackstaff Press
an imprint of Colourpoint Creative Ltd
Colourpoint House
Jubilee Business Park
21 Jubilee Road
Newtownards BT23 4YH

Printed and bound by CPI Group UK Ltd, Croydon CRO 4YY

A CIP catalogue for this book is available from the British Library

ISBN 978 1 78073 234 3

www.blackstaffpress.com

Some names and identifying details have been changed
to protect the privacy of individuals.

To those who served through so
many very dark days. I feel great pride in
having worn the same uniform.

Contents

A note from the author

I joined the Northern Ireland Fire Brigade not because I wanted to be a fireman but because my mother told me to get a job – I'll be forever grateful to her for the push. I was excited to report to Central Fire Station in Belfast on 6 April 1981 and I immediately knew this was somewhere I was going to enjoy. Almost as quickly, I realised I'd be working alongside some very brave people. These 'auld hands' had many years in the job, with the wit, the savvy and, in some cases, the scars to prove it. It didn't take long to realise it was a privilege to serve alongside them. Thirty years later I hung the boots up and knew even more deeply how much of a privilege it had been.

It's therefore been an enormous honour to gather the stories you are about to read and I am humbled by the knowledge of how little I endured compared to many others. Some of the incidents that are recounted remain difficult for the tellers – even, in some cases, nearly fifty years on – so it was important to me that they should tell their stories in whatever way they wished. Most chose to chat about those experiences, often shedding tears and sharing laughter over tea and buns, whilst others wanted to reflect and take time to write down their words. The ways in which the stories were told may not be obvious as you read, but you will definitely get a sense of how different the contributors are. As firefighters and control room staff, we reflect the broader community we come from but we are individuals and we speak in our own ways. What gives us our shared identity is pride in having served in this often bruised and battered firefighting service. You might, if you spent long enough trying, find someone who wishes they hadn't joined – but you'd have to work brave and hard to track them down. The rest of us can't believe our good fortune to have been a part of it.

Introduction

This book sets out to bring to a wider audience the experiences of the firefighters who served in Northern Ireland during the Troubles.

Most firefighters were either full time or retained, but a small number served in both parts of the service. It was also the case that officers often moved to different areas on promotion. As a result, you will see that some individuals share stories from different towns and different parts of the service. In a small number of cases, we also hear two people talking about the same incident. What is striking about these recollections is that even though two firefighters were at the same event, they have been left with different memories and experiences.

Although there is a discernible thread that runs through many of the recollections in this book – that many would have wanted more mental health support – this is not a universal view. What *can* be stated without any qualification is that it would undoubtedly have been better if supporting services had been available sooner for those that needed them. Given the evidence that some people's mental health was affected by the work. many place the blame for this with senior managers who 'didn't understand what the troops had to do'. I do not know about other agencies, but I believe that to suggest this in the specific case of the fire service would be unfair.

Clearly, during the 1970s and 80s there was no obvious appreciation by senior managers of the emotional and psychological impact that such brutal and violent experiences could have on individuals – but this wasn't because they were so-called desk jockeys. In the fire service we have a long and proud history of everyone – up to and including the chief fire officer – being operational: we all respond to emergency calls and fight fires. Certainly the frequency of this work declines with promotion into the most senior posts, but en route to those roles, everybody experiences the coal face. If anything, it's more likely that these senior officers didn't even grasp the harm being done to their own mental health and felt a huge pressure to look like they were strong leaders and were coping. Irrespective of the truth of this particular issue, whilst many firefighters have survived their Troubles experience without particular damage to their mental health, many did suffer, and sadly continue to do so.

A fire station crew is no different from any other group of people in Northern Ireland and reflects the religious and political mix of the local population. Although there may often be a clear majority from one community, every station is made up of a mixture of people from different backgrounds. Even in the worst days of the Troubles, the varied and often strongly held political beliefs that firefighters had were left at the door. When we put on the uniform we were all firefighters and we took pride in doing our job without fear or favour. When situations were dire, we pulled together, and while Northern Ireland was being ripped apart by sectarian divisions, we watched out for each other as if those differences didn't exist.

Much has been written about the Troubles and there is some literature on firefighters working in particular locations, but this collection of very personal and powerful stories covers the whole country, with contributions from full-time, retained and control room staff. It has been impossible to perfectly align some of the terminology used with more contemporary language and, in particular, the use of both the words fireman and firefighter is common.

Some contributors share a number of stories that run to many pages whilst others may share just one or two. Some are light-hearted but most are serious, and some are hard to read. The aim of the book is to try to give a reader who has no particular knowledge or awareness of the fire service a real sense of what it was like to serve during the Troubles and to illustrate the challenges that it presented for firefighters and the impact it had on them.

The number of people who served during this period – from those who joined the service years before 1969 but caught the first few years, through to those who joined in the mid- to late nineties and saw the tail-end of the violence – is perhaps two or three thousand. With just over thirty contributors, this book therefore represents a tiny sample: it scratches the surface. Hopefully it does so in a way that does justice to the thousands of others who could not contribute.

This is a sincere attempt to honour the service of all those who put on the uniform, putting on the record their experiences for the wider community to understand and share.

Undoubtedly for many responders – and firefighters are but one group – the experience of serving in the Troubles was, as one contributor puts it, 'a mixture of terror and excitement'. Most of us survived, most of the time, but for some, the deep and unerasable marks stayed with us. That fact acknowledged, there's no one I have met who – if they had the choice again – would not put on the uniform and serve.

The engine room in Central Fire Station, Belfast, 1988.

The Fire Brigade during the Troubles

When the Troubles kicked off there were two fire services in Northern Ireland. The Belfast Fire Brigade, funded and operated by Belfast City Council, provided the firefighting response within the city's boundary. Everywhere outside Belfast was under the control of the Northern Ireland Fire Authority. Belfast only had full-time staff, whilst the Fire Authority had mainly retained staff, with a single full-time station in Derry/Londonderry. Although they were operating to the same UK standards and traditions, there were differences and the relationship between the two sets of senior managers was cordial rather than overly close. The Troubles were a big shock to the system for both services and – following a broader move to local authority amalgamations in Great Britain and Northern Ireland – the two services were merged: the Northern Ireland Fire Brigade came into being in 1973. With its headquarters in Lisburn, the new service strained as it contended with the amalgamation and the huge workload that the Troubles continued to bring. But despite that challenge, frontline staff continued to get out on the trucks and do the job that the community desperately needed them to do.

The fire service uses a rank structure both for operational 'incident command' functions and for day-to-day management. As a firefighter is promoted up through the ranks they are slotted into the emergency response at different levels: the more senior they are, the larger and more serious the incidents they attend. Although it has evolved over the years, it is still essentially the same today. Most fire service resources – and in particular the firefighters themselves – got to the incident on the fire engine, which carried (in most instances) a crew of between four and six. It also brought the essential firefighting equipment: a large built-in water pump, hose, ladders, rescue equipment and breathing apparatus. There were also specialised appliances, including the high-reach 'aerial' trucks that allowed one or more firefighters to work at heights of up to thirty metres off the ground. At the start of the Troubles the fire engines had bells rather than sirens, then the familiar-sounding 'two-tone' horns were fitted before, in later years, an electronic siren or 'wailer' became standard. The fire engine crew had as its officer-in-charge either a leading fireman or a sub officer, the latter being the more senior.

Above a particular rank, officers respond to fire calls in a fire service car. These are normal cars with no additional protection and – until very recently – only identifiable as fire service vehicles by a blue light and limited signage on the roof. In some circumstances, cars were mistaken for police vehicles, with serious consequences. These officers went to incidents on their own and, if they were on their 'standby' time, they left from and returned to their own home. That duty system – originally called the 'residential' system – was adapted to the 'flexible duty system' many years ago. For many who worked it, the word flexible was usually – jokingly – taken to mean that the officer needed to be 100 per cent flexible as they went where and when they were sent, often to the point of exhaustion. One particular characteristic of that system was that, while the crew in the fire engine could chat about the incident – both as they drove back and when they got to their station – the officers had a more solitary existence. It's not possible to state with any certainty that these officers suffered more as a result of that lack of informal support, but it is hardly a stretch to speculate that they might have.

Full-time firefighters worked a shift system to cover the 24/7 needs of their station. A typical day included the testing and maintenance of essential equipment, practical training (or drills) and fire safety work. The crews were always in a state of readiness and – except when practical training involved having a lot of equipment off the truck – the time it took to get the fire engine out the door when a fire call was received was consistently well below one minute.

At the start of the Troubles this full-time cover was managed using a three-watch system and, in the late seventies, by the addition of a fourth watch. The original watches were Red, White and Blue and the fourth one, when it was created, was called Green. Although this might sound like some play on the politics of Northern Ireland, it was in fact simply the naming convention used in the rest of the UK. The day shifts were nine hours and the night shifts fifteen. Because these ran across weekends, firefighters were regularly off-duty in the middle of the week and many had day-off jobs that they could work around these shifts. Pay was generally considered to be poor but in 1977 a strike brought improved pay and a reduction in hours (hence the additional watch). It's fair to say that, although it was a steady and secure job, you didn't join to become rich.

The retained service had a long and proud history even before the Troubles came along. Recruited locally to serve locally, these firefighters were on call and normally had a full-time occupation as well as their fire service one. Personnel received an annual 'retainer' for making themselves available for firefighting – hence the name – as well as receiving a turnout fee for attending calls and a drill night fee for their weekly training commitment. Because the firefighting workload could vary considerably between the larger towns and the smaller villages, the number of calls an individual firefighter attended also varied hugely. That said, regardless of where you served, over time you would experience the best and the worst that the job would bring – and with the Troubles this shared experience extended to every station and every firefighter.

When the Troubles started, stations were mobilised by different means, including civil defence air-raid-type sirens often located on the local police station roof. Slowly they were all brought into a more technically advanced system that was completely under the fire service's own control. Sirens remained for many years the principal means of alerting a crew, but this was augmented towards the end of the seventies by radio pagers. In the late eighties the sirens, to the dismay of many, were taken out of service and thereafter the firefighters were mobilised exclusively by these pagers.

For retained firefighters, one of the most challenging things about this system was the need to have a supportive employer. The fire brigade would check if the boss in their full-time job was willing to let the prospective retained firefighter drop everything and run out the door for a fire call – at any time of day. While many employers were unwilling, enough could be prevailed upon to enable the service to function – and we are perhaps not appreciative enough of the absolutely critical nature of that goodwill.

The chief's inspections were an annual ritual that aimed to ensure firefighting standards remained high. The station would practice set-piece drills and clean the fire engine and its equipment to the best possible level of spick and span. The chief would inspect the crew and their kit, the fire engine and its gear, and then watch the crews perform their practical drills. Afterwards there was usually a bit of a pep talk followed by an off-the-record chat at which the station personnel could have a bit of a gripe session.

At full-time stations these inspections were taken seriously, but perhaps treated with a degree of detachment. At retained stations the personnel would spend the preceding weeks cleaning their truck and kit like they were expecting a royal visit. This difference is largely explained by the simple fact that retained firefighters regarded the station and the fire engine as *theirs*, whereas at a full-time station with its different watches, this connection was a little less personal. It is certainly true that the effort put into cleaning at a retained station was generally greater – though some full-time folks would, with a little cynicism, have speculated that this was usually a good way to distract the chief from other potential issues ...

It is a temptation to gloss over the challenges the service faced internally during the Troubles, but honesty requires that acknowledgement is made of the, at the time, long-running dispute between the Fire Brigades Union and senior management over the payment of 'danger money'. The union argued that firefighters in Northern Ireland were doing a job that was very different from their colleagues in Great Britain both in terms of workload and level of danger. The dispute ran for some time and, in due course, involved the national leadership of the union and the TUC. Significant political pressure was brought to bear and eventually agreement was reached. As a result, a 'Northern Ireland allowance' of £4 per week was established for full-time personnel with a pro rata payment for retained staff. Even allowing for the effects of inflation, this wasn't a princely sum but it was quite an achievement at the time and the local (Region 2) Fire Brigades Union officials could be justly proud.

While the neutrality of firefighters was generally respected, it wasn't by any means as simple as that – all too often they were collateral damage. They were also directly targeted with whatever came to hand when there was street violence. Deaths did occur – including one by shooting and a small number as a result of bomb explosions – but it almost defies belief that more firefighters were not killed or seriously injured when they were doing such high-risk work so frequently. We frequently joked (half-joked, that is) that we had angels on our shoulders – and it certainly often felt that way.

But being on the receiving end of aggression was sadly all too routine and, fairly quickly after the Troubles started, the fire engines became targets for bricks, bottles or anything that could be thrown. Appliance windscreens were regularly smashed and equipment stolen off the vehicles. Although this was most acute in Belfast and Derry/Londonderry, it happened almost everywhere. Over time, the appliances were modified to provide some additional protection for the crews – plastic windscreen inserts and plastic side windows, for example. Some appliances became so pock-marked that we often referred to them – using a well-known TV ad line of the time – as being like Tetley tea bags: covered in hundreds of little perforations. Certainly they looked like nothing else in the United Kingdom or Ireland. As the Troubles waned, we still had some of these appliances in service and if we had visitors over, we always made a point of taking them to the stations that had one of these tea bags – it usually got a response!

It is also appropriate to acknowledge that the style of firefighting commonly deployed during the Troubles would probably not be tolerated today. Risks were taken that in the current world of health, safety and risk assessment would be deemed unacceptable. This is not to suggest that today's firefighters never take risks – of course they do – rather, that the world today is different and, right or wrong, we were more aggressive in how we dealt with things back then. I am sure that most of us who served during these times would still think that we got that high-risk approach generally right, while admitting we did make mistakes and had the advantage of less public scrutiny. Acknowledging that – and allowing for the effects of sentiment and nostalgia – it stills feels inherently right that those risks were taken.

The control room in Fire Brigade HQ, Lisburn, 1986.

THE CONTROL ROOM

At the start of the Troubles, fire service resources were mobilised by three control rooms: Derry/Londonderry, Lisburn and Belfast. The Fire Authority had responsibility for the both of the controls outside Belfast, while the Belfast Fire Brigade had its own mobilising facility at Central Fire Station on Chichester Street. Using a combination of what might nowadays seem rather technically basic systems, the personnel who worked in these rooms managed – through incredibly busy and difficult times – to get the fire engines and the firefighters out the door. As time progressed these systems were modernised and streamlined. By 1974 there was one control room for all of Northern Ireland at the headquarters of the newly formed Northern Ireland Fire Brigade in Lisburn.

At the start of the Troubles the control rooms were staffed by (male) firefighters but in the early seventies a decision was taken to employ female control operators so that the firefighters could be put on the trucks. As a result, since then, the control room has had a majority of female personnel. Until more recent times, controls had their own rank structure but now those various ranks have the same title as their operational colleagues.

The principal role of the control room is to take all calls for fire service assistance, identify the appropriate resources and mobilise them. The vast majority of these emergency calls come through the 999 system but some also come via the police and ambulance controls. Once appliances are dispatched, the control room maintains radio contact with the incident commander on the ground and handles any requests from them for additional resources. As well as these essential functions, controls also keep senior officers informed of any significant incidents and handles any initial media enquiries.

The control room was – and remains – the nerve centre of the service. While individual crews know the detail of the incident they are attending, the control room knows about all emergencies being attended across Northern Ireland.

Radio procedures were developed to improve the efficiency and clarity of communications. Fire engines and senior officers were given call signs and a small number of acronyms and codes were developed to further assist the service. Thus we might be mobilised to a 'suspect 7/7' and would know that this was a suspected bomb. In the days when any domestic radio user could tune into radio frequencies used by the emergency services, these NI-specific phrases were designed to make it harder for anyone eavesdropping to understand what we were attending or what we were doing. In later years, there was a move to a frequency not normally found on consumer radios, and then, later still, a migration to a sophisticated digital radio system that couldn't be received by anyone but the service itself.

As the first point of contact for the public when they need the fire brigade, the control room personnel hear the strain in the voices of people in various states of anxiety. This can range from being relatively low-level when, for example, the caller is reporting grass on fire along the roadside, to the absolute panic of someone trapped in their home in fear of death. Like their colleagues in the police and ambulance services, the operators handling these distressing calls have both a particular skill and very real emotional resilience.

Heather Magowan
Joined the full-time service as a control operator in 1972.
When I first joined we were called firewomen because we were the first women to come into the service – we were treated as firewomen in the control room. The firemen were originally in there taking the fire calls, and the bosses decided to move them out to put them on the fire appliances, so they brought us in to take over that position. So three of us started in the Lisburn control room and three started down in Belfast because it had its own fire brigade. For the first

few months we were sent to Belfast to try and learn Belfast Fire Brigade's system – we had to take it in turn to go down every so many days to their control room. One week down there and one week up in Lisburn. That was an eye-opener. When I first started at Lisburn there was a switchboard – you pulled the plug out and pushed it in. Then we went down to Belfast and they were modern. They had *keys* – because Belfast was the top!

There would often be attacks on the courthouse next door to Central Station, and that meant that the place had to be evacuated. You would see all the appliances going out to their various spots and then we would have to run out. The very first time this happened when I was there, a very nice fireman called Jock who used to work in the control room handed me this big pile of files and said, 'Heather! Run!' and I said, 'Run? Where to?' So he said, 'Out to the staff car!' We'd jump into a staff car and race off to what they called the shadow control room. We raced through the traffic, at what to me seemed like tremendous speed, because I was so nervous. When we arrived at the other end he took me by the arm and he said, 'C'mon, Heather,' and he led me into the control room, and says, 'Just sit there.' I sat with the files. Eventually he turned round and he gave me a cup of tea and he said, 'Sure you're all right – you're gonna be okay.' I was so scared – and that was my first impression of the Troubles in Belfast!

But fairly quickly I learned how to take fire calls. A call comes in – the board is set out that so many lines are your responsibility. Then the next operator has so many lines, and then so many lines for the rest of Northern Ireland. The line would flash – you would put the key down, say 'Fire Brigade', and then start to ask questions. Usually the person's voice will tell you whether it's really serious or whether it's something minor. You can also tell by the voice what part of Northern Ireland the caller is from, because Northern Ireland has five or six very strong accents. So that helps you pin down too where they are from. As you're asking the questions sometimes, maybe, you don't ask something important, and your supervisor behind will be saying to you, 'Ask them X.' So, you're listening to the caller, you're asking questions, you're listening to your supervisor behind, and you also have the radio operator beside you who's maybe dealing with other calls. You're just listening all around and trying to take information in. At the same time you're writing, and so you had to have your own code because the person was talking fast in fright, or worry, or fear. You had to write quick to try and get all the information down. You really started to listen to voices and be able to deal with two or three jobs at once. There was such a mixture of calls, you never really knew what you were going to get when you answered a fire line, which maybe made it more nerve-racking because you just weren't sure what was going to come your way.

Working in the control room, voices became very important. You had that voice on the end of the phone: the 999 call. You had the voices of everybody in the room. And especially on the radio. The radio used to alert you to the different voices and the tones, and how the firemen were reacting. The urgency of the voice, the quicker it got, the higher it got. In a way you knew them … but you didn't actually know them because we had times when an officer would walk into the control room, and he would stand and smile at you, and we would all turn and look at him, and go, 'Who is it?' Then he would speak and we would go, 'Oh, that's divisional commander such-and-such, or whoever it was. We'd recognise the voice, but didn't know the face. You knew the voice really well on the phone, and you had your idea that this was a really nice man, and maybe that he was six foot – and then he came in and he was five foot five. You know how you can imagine somebody by their voice? I'm sure the firefighters were the same. They must have looked at us and went, 'Now which one did I speak to on the phone?' Then you spoke and they'd recognise you too.

In those days, when the call was finished and you got the okay from your supervisor on which appliance you were going to send out, you then had to relay the information that you had gathered. You would flick the key down of whichever station it was, and you would set off their harmonics. Then, over the station speakers, you would give them the address of the property they had to go to. You'd give this three times. The next thing you would hear would be the appliance booking out on the radio. Once the appliance went out you could give them more details. So you would pass your pad over to the person on the radio, and you would say to them: it is the second house on the right, and it's got a white door, a red door, and it all helps the firemen.

Shortly after I joined they brought in a card system – every street in Belfast was on a card. The card gave the name of the street, and then underneath it gave the main road. It was on a colour system so that you could look at that. You would have seen the station name and you could also see then which appliance would go to a call. If it was a small fire, you had to make a decision about what appliance went to it. If it was a bigger call two appliances went. If it was a building where they needed a turntable ladder then you made that choice and that meant a second station, maybe, going with the original first one. At the time we thought it was really modern and we were very impressed with the system. It did make life much easier, but then, as things change, you become computerised and you look back, and you think, 'Wow! How things have moved on.'

I always remember one evening and there was a lot of bombing going on. We nearly had every appliance in Northern Ireland out and with calls like that the first crew need a relief crew so you'd be pressing buttons and hoping that the retained would be able to turn in and give you another crew. They had to manage so much because they worked during the day, and then they were turned out to calls – they were under a lot of pressure. They really tried their best, but sometimes you were pressing buttons and there just wasn't the crew there. So it was a balancing act to try and keep all the stations covered, yet you had to try your best to remember who had been out for five or six hours when you'd only been home for two hours to get some sleep – you had to remember all that as well. I think the thing was it all had to be done so quickly. That was the main factor.

You can't pinpoint an actual day or week as being the busiest ever because there was quite a long time during the Troubles when one day followed into another into another. A night duty was the worst time because there could have been more bombing in the evening time or at night time – but I think it brought us all closer together as a team because we all tried to help each other as much as possible.

One night duty we received a call down to the border, so we turned out an appliance and Jackie Kennedy, the station officer at that time. They came up behind an army patrol, who were maybe going to the fire call as well, and the next instant Jackie's voice came over the radio saying that they were under fire. You could hear by his voice – plus the sound that we now realised was gunfire and the shouting and the yelling of the army and the retained. He told us afterwards that they all had to jump out of their vehicles and get into a ditch as the gunfire was coming across the top. His voice was always unique – a nice strong voice – and you could hear it all in the sound of his voice, how much was going on around him. But he was very calm, he came back on, and in his usual, calm, matter-of-fact voice said, 'We were under fire there, but we all walked away from it.' He was a really nice man, and had a lot of experience.

We had a police PW – a 'private wire' – coming into the control room. When you answered that you knew that most of the time it was going to be a serious call. Sometimes it was just the police checking on earlier calls – maybe giving updates on the situation or asking us for information on what the firemen had given back to us over the radio. Or it could mean that something quite serious had happened. In the control room you could tell sometimes with the calls that were coming in how it affected the members of staff because they would go quite quiet and they would be thinking too about their own loved ones outside – where they were. You must remember that we were all so young – from eighteen to mid-twenties – and it was quite an experience to be getting these calls that might be about fatalities or casualties. After you'd had a busy day or night duties, you would have gone home and definitely had to talk to whoever was at home. You would have talked to them about different things that had happened. Usually they smiled and nodded and said, 'oh dear!' – they didn't really understand the facts or what you were trying to relay to them, because we were in a very unique position and we were very much cut off from the outside world in many ways. Yet you were getting all this brought to you. I think we had to talk to *somebody* about it. I know a lot of people said, 'You either eat for comfort or you don't eat for comfort!' and I think that was true of everybody in the control room. We all had ways of dealing with stress and coping with what we had heard or been told by the men out on the ground who must have suffered terribly too.

Most people in the control room tried to tune in on the radio operator and to what was coming over on the radio, because when the firemen arrived at a fire, they sent information – you were trying to listen to that. If you had originally taken the call you wanted to hear what was happening on the ground and you tried to listen in on the radio operator to get all the information possible. I do remember that people would have been out on their tea break, and they would have come up to hear what happened regarding a call that they had taken because it was a bomb or something really terrible. They just wanted to know if the men had got there and were dealing with it and what the news was. That happened quite a lot: people came up to stand beside the radio and hear the outcome.

At extreme, busy times, you would have had the keyboards all flashing. There would have been lights flashing and the tone of the fire call coming through, so it would mean that every position was taking a call. Even the supervisors had to step in because there were so many calls. If the incident was in a heavily-populated area or it was something really big, a lot of people rang the fire brigade, which was good, but it also meant that you were getting numerous calls for the one problem or the one call. It meant you had all this noise going on. You have to bear in mind that there were two radio positions: one dealt with the Belfast area and the other for the country, so you had normal calls going on, and you would have both radios going. On top of that, you'd have admin calls, which would be calls from officers looking for information, the police asking for an update on a previous call, often the press. So you had many noises going on. You had to zoom in on what you were dealing with – which is something that you had to learn, how to concentrate on one thing but maybe listen to something else that was going on too. You worked as a team. You were looking sideways because you knew the person beside you was taking the same call and you were trying to see if they had got the same details, and maybe they had got a bit more, which had to be given to the radio operator. You just had to be constantly observant and aware.

Gerry Stafford
Was based throughout her career in the control room at brigade headquarters in Lisburn.
I started in the Northern Ireland Fire Brigade in June of 1974 and my position was then a fire control operator. That meant I took the fire calls coming in on the 999 lines and mobilised the appliances to the incident. When I started, there wasn't all the fancy equipment that they have now – it was all done

manually, whereas today it's all automated. When I started in the job, when a fire call came in, we had to answer and say 'Fire Brigade', and that meant just pushing the switch down where the red light was flashing and speaking into your headset as clearly and calmly as you possibly could. Hopefully that maybe put the caller at ease right from the start. So you would have said 'Fire Brigade', and hopefully the caller would have said, for example, 'My chimney's on fire at 21 Lisburn Road.' We would have said, 'Right, thank you very much,' and told them the fire brigade was on their way before hanging up. There was a box to the right-hand side of the radio operator in the old control room that had all the Belfast addresses in it in alphabetical order, thank goodness, and you would pull out the card for the Lisburn Road. The card would tell us which station was to be mobilised and we knew that a chimney fire only required one appliance. The Lisburn Road would have been Cadogan Fire Station and we would have mobilised them. Then the appliance, when it was pulling out from the station, would have come through on the radio and said, 'Cadogan One mobile to 21 Lisburn Road, Belfast,' and you noted the time of that on your half-sheet where you had taken down the address. The radio operators also did the same thing and passed that half-sheet to me. When the appliance booked in attendance at the fire the same thing happened: you noted the time. The next thing, hopefully, would have been a stop message to say that the fire was under control, and no further action was required. Then when they were finished and the appliance was ready, Cadogan One would have booked mobile back to station. We had to write all that down on a half-sheet and then transfer it to what was called an incident sheet. All that information went on to it: the address of the call, the station that was turned out, the appliance that was turned out, the time that the call came in, the time that the appliance went out, the time that the appliance got in attendance, the time that the firefighters got the fire under control, and then the time that the firefighters booked back to their station. Then the incident sheet was passed to the officer in charge who checked it and signed it at the bottom.

Anybody in Northern Ireland that dialled 999 and asked for the fire brigade came through to our control room in Lisburn headquarters in Castle Street in Lisburn. And the caller could have been anywhere, from Portrush to Newry and everywhere in between. The control room answered all the fire calls for the whole of the north of Ireland, and sometimes for calls in the south of Ireland. That was fun, because their chief fire officer sometimes wasn't even aware that our fire appliances had been in his area. We had to ring him up and say, 'We had a turn-out to a fire at the Holyrood Hotel in Bundoran,' and he would have said some choice words like, 'Why would you not let me know before?' And we would have said, 'Well, we assumed that your system works the same as ours, so you would have got the call, or your control system would have got the call and turned out the appliances to the hotel.' But anyway, that was how it was dealt with.

We had to have a minimum of eight people in the control room. There were two radio positions: one at the left-hand side of the console, and one at the far right of the console. In between was where all the fire calls were taken. The supervisors were at a console behind the operators and there were normally two supervisors on duty. There was a fire control officer, a senior fire control operator and a leading fire control operator. Normally it was the senior and the leading fire control operators who were at the supervisors' desk, unless they were on a tea break, or a lunch break, or whatever and then the fire control officer would have to take up that position.

In front of the operators was a board that showed the various divisions and their stations. When the operators turned out the appliances, the board lit up with the station that was out at the call and if it was mad busy – I mean, sometimes it looked like Christmas – it was all lit up with big red dots. You could tell at a glance how busy we were – that's how we knew. But the firefighters in the station can't see that board. I used to say to the firefighters that when we turn them out, they're going out to deal with 1 call – but in the control room we could be dealing with 101 calls. So, it might not be possible for other operators, or your supervisors, to come and help you with your call – it just depended on what was going on at the time.

Ascertaining exactly where help was needed was one of the challenges for the control room staff.
Calls also came in from rural areas and, if anybody has ever driven round Northern Ireland they will know there are plenty of rural areas, and little lanes that go up to houses and farmers' barns and all kinds of things that you don't see from the road. And unless the person making the call knew exactly where the incident was – the official address, that is – it could have been a struggle to try and get the information we needed. First of all you would have asked them, 'What's the nearest town?' and hopefully they would have given you their nearest town. Well, then you pinpointed that on a map and you would have said, 'Well, what's your nearest main road?' and you hoped that they would give you a name that was on the map. And you could say, 'Right, yes, and how far along that road are you? How many miles are you from the town on that road?' and hopefully they would have given you roughly the number of miles. 'Have you got a house number?' – and, while this was all going on, they could have been screaming, 'Hurry up! Hurry up! Get the fire brigade out! My house is on fire!' You had to try and keep the person calm, and you did that by reassuring the person that the fire brigade was on the way, because by this time you had a rough idea, probably, where the caller was, and you had an idea which station you had to turn out, so you mobilised that station. The men were on their way but you're still giving

them information when they were en route to the call.

I was made up to a leading fire control operator about the end of 1975. And then in 1976 I was made up to senior fire control operator. And I was quite chuffed with myself – I had never had a job like this before. I mean, I had been a telephonist in previous jobs, but I had never dealt with emergency calls. Sometimes it was quite daunting when your fire control officer was off duty and had left a note saying, 'Gerry, you're going to be in charge of the watch tonight.' So if anything went wrong, it was totally on my shoulders. If the wrong appliances were turned out, if the wrong officers were turned out, if they weren't turned out at all – yes, that was my fault.

I think we had one of the biggest mobilising areas in the United Kingdom, bearing in mind that there were only six full-time stations in the country – five of which were in Belfast and one of which was in Londonderry – and the rest were retained. So, you could say that the majority of the calls were rural calls and they could be the most difficult to handle because you had to constantly be at the map, and, you know, it wasn't a great map. We had a bigger one at the bottom end of the control room, but the supervisors' map wasn't all that big, so we had a magnifying glass that we used to get out, and we couldn't see the names too clearly on the map. But we managed – we coped. The operators were great. We worked together, you may as well say, twenty-four hours a day. It was like a family. We took our breaks together and if it got busy we had bells to ring to alert those people that were down, maybe having lunch or tea or whatever, that they were needed back up in the control room and they would come flying back in.

In the seventies, when I joined, and up into the early eighties, during a night-time or even a day shift, the map could have been completely lit up. We had to turn out to the bomb scares and to explosions where there had been no warning or anything … It did affect you because you took the call and you thought … We would often have got those calls not from the public, but from the police. And you maybe would have thought, a bomb has gone off and nobody got any warning. And, how many people are in that building? Are they all right? Can they get out? So it was quite scary at times.

There was a heatwave during the summer of 1976 that made the control room staff's shifts busier still.

The summer of 1976 was a very memorable one for me – we were very busy with gorse fires and forest fires. We had appliances everywhere in Northern Ireland out to grass and gorse fires. Maybe all of the whole-time stations in Belfast were out dealing with bomb scares or explosions. The same applied to Londonderry. They could have had an appliance out at a grass fire but the next thing then – boom, here's a bomb. So you've got to get somebody else to go to the grass fire and try to get your whole-time men back to the bomb explosion. To say you got used to it would be sort of wrong, but it would be sort of right too. You took it in your stride. You got on with your job, that was your job. You took the call. You mobilised the appliances. You listened to the messages coming in. And sometimes the messages were horrendous. Especially when people had been blown up, and, you know, firemen were picking up parts of their bodies. And I think maybe people would have seen that happening on television.

Especially, although it wasn't in 1976, the likes of the Oxford Street Bus Station bomb. I've friends who were on duty that day and I mean, it went off, and it … I mean the people were just blown … You can imagine … You take a call saying that Oxford Street Bus Station has blown up. And there are hundreds of people injured, or dead. Well you can just imagine a group of people standing, waiting for a bus to come in, to go home to their loved ones and the next thing bang! And they're … these people are demolished. They're split apart. Their families don't know it yet – but we knew it. And it did pull at your heart strings. But you've got to get on with it. Because if you didn't get on with it, what would happen? What would happen to those people? As I said, the firemen went out, and they were dealing with one call. But we could maybe have had twenty calls like that, when you had people injured in a bomb explosion. In the control room people would have been sitting at their positions with tears running down their faces. I shed the odd tear myself. But that was reality.

During that dry and busy spell in 1976 we were averaging seven fire calls a minute to grass fires. I was fortunate enough to have a week off, and my husband and I went to the Isle of Man. When you join the fire service you become part of a family. So, when you go somewhere different you think, I'd like to go and see what's going on here. So I dragged my husband along to the headquarters in Douglas and we went into their control room, and there were two gentlemen standing in what was their control room. I got out my pass for the Northern Ireland Fire Brigade and showed it to them, and said that I would like to see around as I worked in the control room back home. One of these gentlemen was a station officer and the other was a leading fireman. They were both standing with cups of tea – not mugs but cups and saucers. I explained to him about how busy we were, averaging the seven fire calls a minute, and his answer to me was, 'Well, we're quite busy at the minute – we've got two calls on. Could you wait a wee minute?' I looked at him, horrified! I said, 'Well that's fine, we'll not disturb you. Maybe we'll come back another day when you're not so busy.' I couldn't believe it. Two fire calls, and two cups of tea with cups and saucers.

There were particularly memorable nights in the control room, and Gerry especially remembers the night of 5 May 1981.
The night that Bobby Sands died, there were lots of calls

to turn out to. Bomb scares across the city. And, of course, the appliances had to be turned out. When the appliances booked an attendance, there seemed to be, especially in the west of the city, quite a gathering of people, who, for want of a better word, abused the firemen when they turned out. Threw anything that they could get at them. They damaged the appliances, broke the windscreens, stole the equipment, and what not. And when you got a radio transmission there was always in the background this noise, this bang–bang–bang, and we later found out that it was everywhere that there had been bomb scares, or incidents where people had required the fire brigade. There were women banging bin lids, just bang-bang-bang-bang-bang-bang. It felt like they never stopped. It was unrelenting, these bin lids, everywhere banging – it was kind of eerie. You know, you were turning men out to … well, you didn't really know what to expect. Dear help them, they probably didn't know what to expect either. We were lucky to be in the confines of our control room, which was protected. But the men were going out and didn't know what they were going to be turning out to. Sometimes they didn't even get an attendance at the incident for missiles being thrown at them. As I say, stones, bricks, buckets, anything, and if they did get an attendance at an incident, people were stealing the equipment off the appliance. I used to think to myself: people doing that, I hope they never have a fire themselves. Because if a fireman turns up with his appliance at an incident and things are missing – it could be something they need to save somebody's life. They were just hard times.

June Smith
Joined the control room in 1972, serving at first in both Belfast and Lisburn before becoming permanently based in Lisburn from 1974.
In the old control room, you had the two radio positions at each end. Then you had position A1, A2, B and C. A2

was Belfast and Dromore and all that; position B was the Cookstown, Magherafelt, Portadown, Armagh areas; C division was basically Londonderry, Dungiven, Omagh – all that area. I was sitting at B position, which was Cookstown. I think it was during break time and no matter what rank you were, you sat in the position where there was a gap. I remember getting a call to Cookstown Fire Station – this man comes on and says he was Father so-and-so, and I said, 'Yes, Father,' and he said there was a house fire out of Cookstown, it could have been on the Orritor Road. I sent the two appliances from Cookstown, and obviously an officer – whoever was on duty. And the next thing was, another call from the police or somebody to say that bombs had gone off in Cookstown. By that time Cookstown had been coming through for information on that first call as to where they were going. They couldn't find anything so I tried to ring that number back and couldn't get through, and that's when we realised that the Father was not a priest – he was there to turn us out with the intention of leaving Cookstown with no fire engines. By that time we had Magherafelt or whoever was the nearest one going to the incident. The bombs had gone off, whether it was one or two, and in fact we did need Magherafelt or Maghera out to it because of the precarious situation of the bomb. But Cookstown were there; they got back in time. After that all hell went off in the centre of Cookstown, and they were laughing at me for calling this man Father when in fact he was a man wanting to bomb Cookstown. He had seemed so genuine and the information that he gave me on the Orritor Road and how far out it was … I was taken in.

I remember a colleague got a call from Derry and the guy said, 'There's a fire in Bishop Street.' In those days, and they probably still do this, you had to ask whether it was within the walls or without the walls. So Donna asked him, and the caller said, 'No, it's coming out the windaes.'

That did not answer the question – she needed to

determine whether the aerial would be able to go to it or not – but where do you go from there? Donna had to think of another way to ask him.

On 16 November 1978 Sub Officer Wesley Orr died in an IRA bomb explosion at a brewery on the Glen Road while he was fighting a fire there.

I always remember Wesley – he was a funny man, but serious. He was the type of guy you never knew when to take him seriously. He used to always look at you; give you that wee expression, and you used to smile back at him because you never knew what he was thinking. Wesley never entered the control room; he stayed in the back yard. You used to see him getting all the hoses ready – Wesley was the hose man. You had to press the button to mobilise Lisburn retained – and that set the siren off in Lisburn. Once the siren went and his alerter went, he got on his bicycle – sometimes he still would have had the pipe in his mouth – raced round to Antrim Street, and hopped on to the machine, away to the incident.

He was always first round at Lisburn Station because he hadn't far to go. And then that day we got a call to the Ulster Brewery, mobilising Lisburn. Wesley went in, I don't know why he went in or what was happening, but as he and his crew were going in to tackle the fire, the second bomb went off and it got Wesley. It came through on the radio that there was a fatality, and if I remember rightly we didn't know who the fatality was; if it was a soldier, policeman, fireman. Then I think someone on another channel came through to say that the fatality was Sub Officer Orr.

I remember that day: it must have come on the radio because there was just a silence in the control room. We were all shocked but, although that was happening, there were various other calls coming through for other incidents. I think that was one of our busiest times for bombs throughout Northern Ireland. No matter what, we still had to go ahead and take a 999 call. Whether it was for a chimney fire, a house fire or something simple, you still had to get on. But you knew in the background the ones that were mobilising, and the ones on the supervisory desk – they were dealing with telling the chief officer and different other people that needed to be told. I think at that time the press were ringing in, looking for information. You had to go on. The shiver that went through us … He was just such a character.

I was at the funeral. It was held in St Paul's Church. We all met outside headquarters. At the service, we were all lined up at the back. The size of the funeral … you couldn't even get near the church. It was absolutely packed out. The amount of uniformed firemen everywhere.

Firefighters Desy Moynes (left), John Nichol (centre) and Gearld McCamley, 1976.

THE SOUTH

Armagh

The cathedral city of Armagh is one of Ireland's most important and historic cities. It is also very close to the border and was greatly impacted by the Troubles. The commercial centre was regularly attacked with bombs and incendiary devices – in many cases, these attacks started huge blazes, often involving more than one premises at a time. The strain on the fire service was immense.

To add to this challenge, when an attack took place in a remote location, the local fire crews that attended often found themselves completely alone or, at best, with little protection. It also meant that the firefighters were making decisions about safety that could only ever be imperfect. In a great many circumstances the firefighters had to take risks to save lives and could only hope and pray for the best.

Desy Moynes

Joined the retained service in Armagh in 1976.

While I was in Armagh in the retained, there was one incident in particular that hit me hard. It was 27 August 1976, about two in the morning, when we got called to a disused greengrocer's. It wasn't a derelict shop, it wasn't a big old derelict building – it was just a business that had failed for some reason and shut. We responded to the station and I was on the second machine – the first pump had already turned out to the fire, which was at 39 Upper English Street, about three hundred metres from the fire station. I recall driving up the street and seeing the flames reflecting in the windows of the businesses opposite. I remember getting out of the appliance and looking at it and the building was, as we call it, 'well alight' on every floor: ground, first, second and out through the roof. I was this greenhorn running around wondering, what am I going to do here? I saw a firefighter – a really, really good firefighter called Brian 'Blue' McArdle, Blue was his nickname – so I teamed up with Blue and he took me up the ladder with him. We were firefighting through the windows, doing our bits and pieces. Eventually we came down and I tied up with Leading Firefighter Knipe – he was working with me on a jet on the ground floor. We started to get the fire beat down and I went into the building. John Nichol and Gearld McCamley were standing inside so I talked to them for a while – they had a hose reel and they were firefighting with that. It was hot and it was steamy, so I said to them, 'Anybody want to take a break?' Gearld said he would, so he walked out across the floor of the shop and on to the street.

I was talking to John about the fire when I heard somebody shouting, really urgent-like – shouting a warning. I turned round and I remember seeing it was Leading Firefighter Knipe. He was silhouetted in the opening of the door and he was shouting at us to get out. I'll not repeat the words he was saying. And that was it: I mean it all happened in seconds, but you could literally hear it coming, you could hear the thud of it on the upper floors. Then the centre of the ceiling just exploded on to the two of us. We were standing side by side and we hadn't even a chance to move – we never had a chance. The ceiling exploded and we got hit. I mean, the force of it hitting us … it pummelled us to the ground. It all happened in seconds.

When it all stopped, I didn't know whether I was upside down – it was like you'd been in an avalanche. I was stunned so I didn't know what was what – I couldn't orientate myself to see what way I was. Then it all stopped and I was thinking, what the fuck just happened there? and then I felt this crushing weight on me. Even though the building had fallen and anybody who was outside thought that it was right down, it hadn't stopped moving because the pile that I was now under was settling: squeezing me and pushing down and down. I was trying to breathe and I couldn't. I couldn't get my chest expanded because of the weight that was crushing me. And, again, this is not happening over a five minute period, this is all in seconds, and I'm still trying to work out what the hell's going on here and then I remember thinking, where's my left arm? I couldn't feel it – I couldn't feel anything from my shoulders down. My arm had got twisted up behind me but then the rubble that was pressing down had cut the blood supply off so it just went dead – it felt like it just wasn't there. Then within seconds my two legs were the same, so I had no feeling. The way I was trapped, my helmet was lodged in the rubble and my head was in it and my chin strap was on and I couldn't even get out of my helmet. I was trapped inside it and the only thing I could move was my right arm – it must have been in a bit of a void somewhere. So I was lying there and I was trying to get my thoughts together: what am I going to do? I was trying to get up as if I could stand up but that was impossible – it wasn't going to happen.

Then the burning started. The building that was on fire was now a pile of roasting-hot rubble and we were under it getting cooked like we were in an oven – that's the only way I can describe it – and the hot bricks, they were jammed into my neck, they were jammed into my back and they were burning into me. It was so black; as black as hell. After a period of time, you sort of just … well, you couldn't panic. I mean, there was nowhere to panic to, so you had to try and get your thoughts together. So I start thinking: right, they are outside and they know we are in here so they will be coming soon to get us. But time went on and went on and nothing was happening. I tried shouting but it was like shouting inside a box, it just wasn't going anywhere, so then I started feeling round a wee bit and I felt something crisp, like crunchy, and I knew it was John's leggings and I knew he wasn't far from me. The two of us were right beside each other. I grabbed his leggings and I started pulling at him and he didn't respond. Even to this day I sort of regret … It's just, even to this day I feel bad about it because I

35

remember thinking, flip, he's knocked out, the bollocks has got himself knocked out here – at least he doesn't know what's happening. I didn't know it then but John was already dead.

So I lay there as there was nothing else I could do and every now and again I would reach out and feel for him and shake him. We just lay and I don't know for how long – half an hour, maybe an hour. I don't know whether I'd passed out with the heat or was just lying there but the next thing I felt was debris hitting me on the side of my face. The first thing that came into my head was, here we go, fuck, this is going to finish us off here. The next thing, this massive blast of cold fresh air came down right above my head. My head was trapped in the helmet so I couldn't look up to see what it was but I heard this voice and recognised it – it was Leading Firefighter Tom O'Kane from Armagh. Trust me, if you were going to be found, he was the guy you wanted to come along – Tom was a bull of a man and I remember Tom shouting, 'I found one, I've found them,' and I was just shouting up at Tom, 'John's beside me, we are here, John's beside me.'

They started working and you could hear them – I mean, you could hear the boys. I started recognising voices: Tony Crilly's, Blue's, Turlough Toner's, Hugh Knipe's, guys that I knew. I remember thinking, they have survived it, they weren't caught in it too, and I was glad of that. They started digging and digging. After a fair while they were above me because of the stuff they had to shift and then, I think it was Tony Crilly shouted down the hole to me, 'There's somebody here wants to speak to you.' I thought, you could have picked a better time, you know, but it turned out it was the local parish priest, Father Richard Naughton.

I actually spoke to him a few weeks ago about it because I hadn't seen him for many years. He told me that he had been in the priest's house and the doorbell had rung and he had got out of bed. He said he knew it was urgent because whoever was ringing the doorbell never let the doorbell go. When he went down, there was a squad of soldiers at the door and they just said to him, 'Father, you have to come with us now. There's been a bad accident.' They put him into the back of the Land Rover and they drove him to the scene. They put a hard hat on him and he went into the building, and for somebody who's not in the fire brigade or anything like that, it was a brave thing for him to do. In the Catholic faith, the Last Rites are the last thing you hear on this earth, so when I'm hearing the Last Rites I'm thinking, Moynesy, you're not in good shape here: these guys know something more than you do. Father Naughton did his bit and was taken out.

The boys started work, pulling away the rubble to get us out. It went on for another while then, next thing – they must have got down fairly close to us – somebody grabbed me by the hand. To feel human contact again when you're in there, it's nice, you know. This guy grabbed me and he says, 'Desy, it's Joe Martin from Portadown.' I'd heard of Joe. I'd never met him before but he was a bit of a legend – years in the fire brigade – and Joe said, 'Well, what are you at the day?' That's firefighters for you because, no matter how dire the situation, they will come out with some crazy comment. I'm sort of thinking, been in better places, Joe, but he held on to my hand and he kept talking away. He was trying to keep my mind off the operation that was going on round us and I kept telling him, John's here, he's knocked out, he's not talking. They dug on and they were working away.

Somebody suddenly said, 'We have to evacuate the building – the rest of it's going to come down.' I always say to people to be very careful when you're rescuing somebody, to be careful what you say. People can hear you. When I heard that, I went, this is it, we're finished. Joe was holding on to my hand and I let go of him – I opened my grip to let him go but he didn't … Joe stayed there and I'm trying to look up at him and he says, 'I'm not going'. I could hear everything – the shouting and the urgency to get people out of the building – and he said, 'No, me and Tom's staying here. We are not leaving you.' It's hard to express it – they were two married men with kids at home – and the both of them made a conscious decision: if that building had come down they weren't getting out of there. They were going to die along with John and me. I mean how do you ...? That's courage.

I think what had happened was that there were so many in working there – extra fire crews brought in and a load of soldiers transported down from the local army base, and everybody was in digging and everybody was pulling – that the building was becoming unstable. So they took everybody out – they were only out for a minute or two – and then they made smaller teams and came in and worked. I gather that's what happened, because I wasn't on the outside looking in.

When it was all over and done with, for years, I always thought, why were those two men, Joe and Tom, never recognised? You know, from a fire brigade point of view, they were never given any recognition for what they did that night and I always ... it made me angry at times. I suppose back then, in the heat of things mixed up with everything else that was going on ... but sometimes I think it's not too late. Sadly both of them have passed away but their families are there and it's never too late in my books to right a wrong: they did what they did and there was never any thanks. I mean obviously whenever it was over I thanked them for it and I worked with them for years after but sadly they're gone. Joe was the last to pass away earlier this year. It was never spoken of again – it wasn't like, 'You owe us a debt.' Joe said to me one time, 'You're a lucky lad,' and Tom said something similar. There was none of the, remember that night we saved you. That was it, done and dusted. I mean, I can't, you can never thank them, you can never thank all of the guys that were there that night. But just for those two guys to do that for me was a special thing.

The days after John's death were traumatic for everybody

in the community, especially in the fire brigade, but in the whole scope of what was happening in Northern Ireland at that time, within hours something else had happened and the news crews were running to that. Within days it all faded out. It was old news ... let's get on to the next. There were bombs going off, riots going off, unfortunately other people were getting killed. It faded into the background.

John was my second cousin. His mother and my father would have been first cousins. John was fire-brigade-mad – he just loved the uniforms, he just loved the fire engines, and when he got his hand on a jet, you couldn't have prised it off him. He was only happy when he was in a fire station or on a call. He was getting his fair share of experience. He was out operational before I was. He had been in a fair few explosions and he had done a good bit of firefighting. His career was cut short at nineteen. He was robbed. I suppose you could say the community of Armagh was robbed too.

That was the nature of the guy, he was just at his happiest firefighting. I suppose in one way he died doing the job he loved. I just happened to be looking it up recently on the Internet, where all firefighters who have been killed on duty are listed, and his name is still on the national memorial at St Paul's in London – so at least he's been recognised somewhere. Often I thought it was a shame too – he was just nineteen; he was a teenager; he is the youngest firefighter to be killed on operational duty in the UK and Ireland since the Second World War, and maybe even during the war – that for some reason he's just been forgotten about and lost. I always thought it would be a great thing for the city council to nominate a schools' trophy or something for community service in his name, but there's nothing – he's just gone and that's it. The local fire station has a memorial to him in the entrance, but from an official point of view, from a community point of view, for a nineteen-year-old lad to lose his life and just to be forgotten about: I think it's a shame. I get a bit angry at that too.

Nowadays they call it survivor guilt, but I could never figure it out. I used to go up to Father Naughton in the priest's house – it was like counselling, just trying to figure it out. I mean the two of us standing beside each other – how it's not a case of John got a broken arm or a broken leg and I got a cut or something like that. You know, he's there and he gets killed and I get a sore left arm. What justice is there in that? I fully understand when you see on the TV, you know, after the Manchester bombing, or you see soldiers coming home from Afghanistan and their colleague was in a Land Rover beside them and was killed and they walk away from it. I know where those people are coming from. It's baggage … and you carry it.

I'm not sure if society understands the job. You hear it said now that when everybody else was running away the fire brigade were the ones going in. That makes great news stories at night and stuff, but there's more behind it than a thirty-second clip of news footage. These guys are living it – not just that incident, but every incident they go to. It doesn't stop when their duty is finished. They are going home. They have families. I don't know how some of the guys back then coped. We certainly didn't bring it all home to our families. You couldn't … but we worked as a team. If you could describe a fire station as a mad house that's what it was. Our counselling was done at the dinner table and when we came back from incidents we talked over a cup of tea and sorted it out ourselves. Back then there was no going to the trauma doctor or anything like that.

A good friend of mine, Firefighter Sammy Gamble, was on White Watch, Central, in Belfast, with me and he would say, 'You remember, Desy, you didn't cause the trouble. You're going to help. It's not your fault and you've got to put it behind you and move on to the next one.' But a year to the night after the incident where John was killed I was in Divis Street in Belfast. It was the same sort of situation: in a building again and the top floor came in on top of myself and another firefighter and it pummelled us down the stairs. I was going, fucken hell – not again. I remember walking outside and there was a divisional officer in Belfast at the time, 'Jonty' Johnstone, and he came over and said to me, 'I understand what you've come through and I know your history. There's my torch – go back in there to the top of that building and disconnect the branch from the hose, the actual branch end, and bring it back to me.' I went back in again, the whole way up through that building on my own, and disconnected it. It was a lonely climb but it was the best thing that ever happened to me – it literally cured me. I had no fear for the rest of my service and I've never had any other bother since it. Probably if Jonty hadn't have done that that night I would have walked away – I'd just had enough of it, but what he did that night set me on my course for the rest of my service. It's just a pity that John didn't get that opportunity. He'd have been a good fireman; he would have been good for the community.

Gerard McKenna

Joined the retained service in Armagh in 1980 and served for twenty-nine years.

Prior to joining the brigade I was an apprentice motor mechanic and I served my time with a local garage close to the fire station. Two of the mechanics in the garage were in the retained, so my interest in the fire brigade was always there from a very young age. It was encouragement from those two men, Owenroe O'Neill and Tom O'Kane, that made me decide to join. These two boys were neighbours of ours at home. It was always a very close-knit family in the retained in Armagh, and I'm sure the same in all stations, because you had two, or maybe three, generations of firefighters in the family. In Armagh you had the Crillys, the Hamiltons, the McArdles and the Stinsons, and they were all three or four generations down the line.

Anyway, a vacancy came up in Armagh and the station officer then, Kenny Millsop, had come over to the garage and he says to me, 'There is a vacancy in Armagh – would you be interested?' The boss says, 'Thanks very much but there's two men in the garage here already in the service and if the sirens go, all three of them would go, and there would be nobody left to carry on with the work.' But I mind Kenny then saying to me, 'Don't you worry about that – if you are interested we'll get the paperwork done and I'll jump that fence whenever we come to it.' That's how the ball started to roll. Later Kenny come over again and he said, 'There's a wee interview organised for you in Armagh Fire Station on the drill night, Monday night.' Charlie Bell was the Divisional Commander in Portadown at the time and he came down for the interview. I can see him yet: he was sitting in the office and there was a glass panel door and I was a shaking bundle of nerves so I was, as I'd never met the man before and there he was, sitting in this regalia. I knocked the door and went in and stood and he says, 'Take a seat there, young man, sit down,' and put me at ease very quickly. He just started to talk in general about me leaving school and being an apprentice mechanic and working with Owenroe and Tom at Pat Kearney's garage. At the time Charlie Bell and Pat Kearney were friends as well and he talked away. Then he says, 'Right, I hear you want to be a fireman.'

I said, 'That's right, sir.'

And he says, 'You know this can be a very dirty job?'

I says, 'Well, could it be any worse than laying under a cattle lorry on a Friday in the cattle market and it all dripping down round you while you try to put a back spring into one of these lorries?'

He started to laugh and he says, 'I believe you have a first aid certificate.'

I said, 'That's right – through the Order of Malta Ambulance Corps.'

He said, 'Well, you are interested in first aid, you are

interested in helping people,' and I said that was right. Then he asked me if I had a driving licence and I said that I did. He asked me if I could drive a lorry and I said that I had been driving lorries round the cattle mart yard on a Friday and the sheep mart on a Saturday and vans and what not in and out of the garage – but that I didn't have the HGV licence. 'That's okay,' he says, 'I will be in touch with you.'

A very short time after, maybe within a week or ten days, Kenny Millsop came over and says, 'There is a letter in the post for you – you'll be starting next Monday night. Be in the station for 19:30 hours.' So here's me, proud as punch up to the station, but the mother and father weren't just so keen on it because of the fact it was in troubled times, and we had already lost John Nichol in Armagh a couple of years prior. When they knew Tom O'Kane was there and Owenroe was there and I was working with them in the garage and we were neighbours at home and they were like father figures to me then as well, that sort of eased things a wee bit. I started on the Monday night and it just took off from there.

With the fire brigade it went from false alarm calls to chimney fires to road traffic accidents to farm incidents, and then into the real sort of serious stuff: car bombs and booby traps and riots. One incident in particular was at the Wellworths store at the junction of Thomas Street and Ogle Street. There'd been incendiaries put in and it was a well-developed fire. We had the ladder extended, jets on the ground floor and jets on the first floor, and all the while this riot was going on between the security forces and the rioters. I'm not sure at that time whether it was plastic bullets or rubber bullets, but they were going at it and we were fighting the fire in the middle of it all. Graham Crossett was the station officer at the time and he was mobilised down to it. As he come round, coming off our street into Ogle Street, the crowd stopped him, hijacked his car and burnt it. The laughable thing about it was, Graham was going for a promotional interview in headquarters the next morning and his uniform and his peaked cap were in the car – and all were lost. To this day it sticks in my mind, Graham later saying, 'I went for an interview for a promotion and it was the first time I hadn't got a peaked cap!' Not a bad excuse, though.

We'd planned a surprise birthday party for my wife Bridie's twenty-first birthday in 1980. We literally only lived round the corner from the fire station – only a hundred metres or so – and with our family and the guys from the station, we were going to enjoy a bit of craic. The next thing I got a fire call. When we arrived at the station they told us it was to John Patrick's drapery store in Thomas Street and it was incendiary devices. When we got there, it was already a well-developed fire and it just escalated. We had appliances from Keady and Portadown. And here's me thinking, all Bridie's relations are coming down and she's in our house and doesn't know what's going on, so I said to the guys when we had the fire rightly under control about coming down home for tea and sandwiches – and of course then everybody, even the Portadown boys, all congregated at the house. Joe Martin from Portadown – God rest the man, a real character – said, 'Get Bridie out on to the street to give her the birthday bumps.' That is a birthday she will never forget. We had to leave the party and go back to the fire again and it was into the small hours of the morning when I got home after that. You were always trying to manage work, family life, work life, fire brigade life – you were trying to juggle them all and keep the peace with everybody.

There were a lot of bombs and big fires in the town. Bombs and incendiary attacks meant that fires would just spring up in various premises and they were usually all-night incidents that went through to the morning – and then you had to go to work afterwards. There was no room for excuses when you were in employment – you had to keep your job going.

Joshua White's car showroom was on the bottom of College Street and we got turned out to a suspect car bomb there. And of course, again, drove past the car bomb to stand by on the opposite side of the Mall. As usual, we shipped the hydrants and ran out hose in preparation. The bomb exploded and the amount of debris and dust and noise was unbelievable. Tom O'Kane was beside me and he said, 'Get underneath the fire engine.' The two of us dived underneath and all the debris was coming down round us. It was a hair-raising incident. Everybody was okay, there was plenty of warning, but the fact was that we drove down past it. Nobody really knew then the high risk or the dangers.

There was one on Scotch Street that was another hair-raising event. We had one appliance standing by in Market Street and I was in charge of the appliance that was standing by in Barrack Street. Scotch Street and everywhere was all evacuated and the army was in attendance. The ATO [Ammunition Technical Officer] said to me, 'Son, if I were you, I'd be getting behind that wall as this is a car bomb and it is well laden-down.' We all took in behind the wall and I mind there had been a pedestrian standing on a wee 'keep left' road island that was a good distance away. I'd seen the flash and this particular man falling to the ground and then there was the unmerciful bang. The guy was actually hit with shrapnel but survived. I couldn't believe the flash, then somebody going down, and *then* the noise.

We also had numerous booby-trap bombs. Again, in them days, whenever you heard an explosion you would be making your way to the fire station before the siren even lifted because you knew it was something serious. This particular day I had heard an explosion and was just turning the key in the fire station door when the siren lifted. Controls told us on the direct line that it was a car explosion at St Luke's Hospital on the Loughgall Road. Arriving down to it, there was a lot of activity, with nurses and doctors and lot of people congregated round a car. The person was fully conscious but was trapped in the car. We managed to extract him from the vehicle but as we lifted him off the car seat, his two legs were left behind. When we got him into the ambulance he was fully conscious, he was able to answer all the questions, and then his legs had to be lifted out of the vehicle and set into the ambulance. He survived and is still living to this day – other people weren't so lucky. We couldn't understand how with amputations like that he was still conscious and able to talk. We heard afterwards – now a medical professional would be able to put this better, but from the way it was put across to us – the force of the blast and the intensity of the heat sort of knitted the nerves and arteries and the blood vessels to prevent massive blood loss.

On 21 January 1981, the IRA killed eighty-six-year-old Sir Norman Stronge and his son James at their home, Tynan Abbey.
That night I was building an engine for a friend when the siren operated and it was a very quick turnout. I was only across the road from the fire station and I was the sixth man on the pump, so it was a quick turnout. Going out to the call we arrived at Tynan Abbey and there was a lot of gunfire at the gates. The army was there and they spoke to the OIC. I couldn't hear the whole conversation, but got the gist of it – that it wasn't a nice call, that there were booby traps, bombs planted at the front door, and there had been gunfire in the area. Going up the avenue we could see that the fire was well developed – you could see the glow behind the glass windows. Because I was very young and a recruit I wasn't a qualified breathing apparatus wearer, but there was a breathing apparatus team sent into the ground floor and it wasn't pleasant for them by any means. The BA team came out and I could see they were carrying a casualty. I ran over to give assistance and Tom came over and, God rest the man, he's dead and gone now too, I mind him saying to me, 'Don't turn him over.' Sometimes when you are told not to do something like that, you do it. I don't know if that is just a natural reaction or not, but I have mind of turning him over and to this day I will never ever forget what I saw.

There was just a person with no face, there was absolutely nothing there at all. We had to lay him down on the ground and what remained of his head was just sort of flowing about as if it was a bit of loose plastic or tissue flapping about. There was no face there whatsoever. I mind laying him down and covering him up.

Somebody said we needed to get a jet so I left and got one, and I put it on to the ground floor of the building. The next thing, it was just like a mass of fireworks going off. Charlie Bell threw me to the ground and the two of us lay on the ground with the jet. It wasn't until after that they told me that the fire had got into the armoury and the ammunition was exploding. We just lay there until the noise died down. But that night in particular I was in daze, like in a trance. I found myself on the roof of the building at one point and I don't know how I got there. For days after it we were constantly returning for dampening down – it went on for days. That was horrendous.

For anyone serving in the fire service anywhere, there is an inevitability about having to routinely deal with horrendous and brutal events. This was amplified by the Troubles and if dealing with 'normal' awfulness is challenging enough, the sheer frequency and scale of Northern Ireland's violence made it all the harder.

I think when I first came into the fire brigade it felt like it was tragedy after tragedy after tragedy. I think I could cope with it because it was happening on a regular basis – nearly daily basis, weekly basis, whatever – and when one tragedy ended, you hadn't really time to think or grieve or talk until another one happened, and there was that much going on back then. We weren't allowed to talk about incidents when we got home – all of that information was confidential. We went to the incident, we dealt with the incident, and when the incident was over we would have gone to the pub, we would've had a drink and we would've talked about it amongst ourselves. There often wouldn't have been anyone else in the pub or in earshot because many's a time a barman would've opened up for us. If we'd had a call early in the morning – a real bad incident – and the barman had still been in, cleaning up from the night before, we might have gone over and tapped the window or tapped the door, and he would have taken us in and set us down the back. We could have talked amongst ourselves but once we left, that was it – there was never any talk at home. I felt I coped with all those incidents over those years. I wouldn't say I was never afraid of going to the next one, but you were in a position, you were there to help, you were there to do your best and you did that, along with your colleagues. You dealt with all those incidents in your own way. At the scene of a bad one, when things are half sorted, I've seen firemen going off in their own wee world or going off to their own wee corner or maybe going for a walk down the road. That happened quite a lot, so it did. There were guys who would've liked a wee bit of quiet time for themselves. But that doesn't always help.

I had one really bad one towards the end of my career when the Troubles had finished. It was to a bungalow up by Seagahan Dam. I don't know whether it was a family feud or that sort of thing, but a fella and a girl got petrol poured over them and set alight and that was not a pleasant sight. That was the one that broke me. Later it was the doctor that said to me that in all my Troubles years I had a big defence – then when the Troubles were over I had this real bad incident and I wasn't prepared for it. My defence was down after that incident. It took me back to the time at Tynan where I had seen the person with no face and here at the dam I had seen this man with no face – there was a mask on over what was left of his face, the paramedics had put the mask on, but you could see the state of him. But it was the girl that I was talking to in the stretcher that really got me. I was holding her hand, trying to hold her hand, but it was so badly burnt – her skin near enough melted – that I couldn't. Afterwards

I thought about it quite a bit, dreamt about it quite a bit and it was really getting to me.

I went to a fatal road traffic accident a short time after. I mind looking at the body and I couldn't touch it and that wasn't me and I knew there was something not right. I wanted to do what needed done but I couldn't and I had to get one of my colleagues to lift the body out of the vehicle. I went back to the station and I started to think, why could I not do that? That was never me, I was always hands-on, I was always there as a sort of a leader. I would never really have asked somebody to do something that I couldn't do myself. I was always hands on in the past but this one I couldn't do. I went home afterwards and thought about it and I couldn't even do my own work, or anything like that. I wasn't focusing at all.

I had fire reports to do and I thought I'd go over to the station to do a couple. Victor Spence, Victor junior, came in and he was all fun and joking, saying it was great to see fire reports getting done and all the rest of it. I mind saying to him, 'Victor, I'm not with it here at all. I came over to get out of the road and try and do something, but something's not right.' Victor saw the serious side of it and asked if I wanted a wee chat. He took me up the stairs and started to talk and I was telling him about the RTC [Road Traffic Collision] and he says, 'Gerard, would you like a wee chat with a doctor? I'm sort of forcing you – I'm not asking you.' He also said that a wee bit of time out mightn't do me a bit of harm. He says, 'You're here twenty-four hours a day, seven days a week – you might need a wee bit of a break, but I can arrange a wee chat with the doctor for you.' He did and I must say that the fire brigade doctor, Dr Jenkinson, he was absolutely fantastic and went through everything with me. He even suggested the trauma centre in Belfast and I met a gentleman there, a retired police officer called Bill, and I had several discussions with him. He talked about his experiences and I talked about my experiences and then he suggested that I have a chat with another doctor, Dr Michael Paterson, a clinical psychologist based in TMR Health Professionals, a company that specialised in treating people with post-traumatic stress. He was really good. All the help that I had from the Fire Service and from the medical professionals and that – it's just ... it's wonderful. You think you're on your own, you think it's the end of the world, but there is help there. I don't know what would have happened to me if Victor hadn't come in at that particular time – it might never have come out and I probably would have sort of battled on and battled on. I don't whether it was coincidence ... maybe it was providence. I still wonder even to this day, if we hadn't had that wee chat in the station, what would have happened. The fire brigade was my life, it was my hobby, my social life. I don't fish, I don't shoot, I don't play golf, I don't have any hobbies – the fire brigade was my life.

Since retiring from the job, I'm busier now than I ever was and that's because I'm looking after our house, maintaining the kids' houses – and doing plenty of car maintenance for them too! I'm enjoying that side of it now. I'm seeing a side of life that I hadn't seen before. I missed my own family growing up but now I'm looking forward to enjoying life with the grandchildren. But truth is, I'd still do it all over again.

Joe McKee

Served in both the full-time and the retained service and was stationed, during different periods, in a number of locations. He has vivid memories of serving in the retained section in Armagh.

In Armagh one night our first two engines had gone to Dungannon and we were waiting for a couple more men to turn up for the third crew when a huge bomb went off in the middle of the town. I remember driving to that incident, and all the people who were coming from the cinema were running in the opposite direction. We drove down Scotch Street and it was like driving down a beach because you could hear the slates and the windows crunching under the wheels. We arrived at quite a small fire, but by the time we had run out enough hose, it was up, up through the roof, and I remember the blue light on the passenger side and the transfer – the sticker, sort of the crest of the brigade on the door – melted in the time that it took me to get up the street to the hydrant and back again.

We used to go a lot from Armagh to Dungannon, to what we call make-ups, to assist them, and again, I remember arriving at the Inn on the Park Hotel in Dungannon in a fire engine from Armagh just as a very large bomb went off. All the Dungannon firemen who had been standing at a safe distance from the hotel actually jumped out over the perimeter wall. It was one of those Keystone Cops memories. That night, the crews walked in and out through the reception area and we actually walked over an unexploded bomb. It was only in the morning when we realised how close we'd been to disaster. There was a sort of miraculous side. When I was chairman of the brigade many, many years later, there was a roll of honour at the door, at the staircase I went up to my office, and I used to look at that every day. Very few of those whose names are on it died as a direct result of the Troubles – though a number did. I often thought, it's a miracle that the list wasn't twice or three times as long.

I suppose of all the jobs I've done – I was involved in education, I was involved in broadcasting, I was involved in the arts – the fire service job was the only job where you could genuinely say that no two days were quite the same.

Joe also attended Tynan Abbey the night the Stronges were killed. Tynan is a village eight miles from Armagh – a very English-looking village, a pretty hamlet with the big house, Tynan Abbey. At the time of the fire, I was teaching in Armagh.

That night I had a form one parents' meeting. I was relaxing afterwards and then I got a fire call. When I responded to the station there were enough guys there already to take the first two vehicles away. I rang my wife, who was a serving police officer – and said, 'I might be late, I think there's a hay fire at Tynan Abbey.' She said, 'No, it's not a hay fire, it's a major incident,' because she had been listening on the radio, and had heard police messages.

I left in the third vehicle from Armagh. There was a gate lodge to Tynan Abbey, and the police were there, and they said, 'You should be careful – we think the IRA are still in the grounds.' That, I have to say, is a great way to focus your attention. We drove through the Gothic-style gate lodge, and as we drove up the avenue we could see our blue lights going round in the trees that were overhanging. The house was not on fire when we arrived, but the recovery of the two bodies from the library was something I shan't ever forget and I know at least one other firefighter in Armagh who found it hard – impossible – to get the vision of that out of his head until the day he died.

There then ensued a large fire, and the building was all but destroyed. It would have been seen for miles I'm sure. It lit up all the grounds – the house had one of those wonderful hedge mazes at the front, and when the big curtains went up in the two-storey main reception room, it lit up the whole garden area. We saved the return at the back of the house, where the housekeeper had left the kitchen table with two places set for breakfast, for Sir Norman and for his son, James. It was beautifully done – nice silverware, napkin rings and so on. That was one of the really sad images of Tynan for me.

My understanding of the events was that a contingent of IRA arrived, I think, at the land steward's house. They were in what looked like military fatigues, allegedly, and, the person in the land steward's house had opened the door and let them in, thinking it was a foot patrol of the British Army.

It was only when they assembled a bomb that they realised. The bomb was detonated and blew off the main front door. I think the Stronges had some sort of a device in the house that they could launch from the roof, a distress flare to alert the local police. That was all done I believe. The police eventually responded. I think the car was surrounded by the unit from the IRA who fired at the car but it was protected, it was armour-plated. There was a helicopter there at one stage. It was a major incident. The people who set out to execute this attack were very successful in what they did. And the fire took hold eventually, but I know from what I saw that the two bodies were recovered from the library as the initial small fire took hold. One chilling aspect was that when the house was full of smoke, two firefighters from Armagh went in with breathing sets and they could hear breathing. It was actually a dog: it was the Stronges' black Labrador that was in the room. So that, of course, was very upsetting to hear, that distressed breathing that they didn't know was a dog. Then to recover the two bodies. Really a very ghastly incident, and the fact that the two individuals were shot at point-blank range, and that others coming on the scene had to confront that and deal with that was very traumatic.

The fire raged a good part of the night. Our chief fire officer, George Morrison, who was held in the highest regard, made his way from Bangor very rapidly. He came round and stood at the end of each hose (the branches as we called them) and talked to each of us. In a way, he did a bit of counselling because he realised this was a major event. We had difficulty with the water – I know we had. The brigade had invested in a new fleet of fire engines at that time and we had new portable pumps, and the intake filter got blocked at one stage. We lost the water supply for a short time but got that back on again quickly. It was a major fire with back-up from stations all round County Armagh as well. I learned too, after I went to do the job as chairman, that Mr Morrison went back into the control room on his way home to Bangor after the fire and thanked the staff in the control room for their contribution. Although they weren't out at the full horror of the event, they had dealt with all the mobilisation and had taken all the assistance messages, and essentially, they had lived through that incident as well, but under the fluorescent lights, if you like, of the control room. I thought it was terrific of the chief to acknowledge the trauma that they had gone through as well. George Morrison did that sort of thing in a most professional way.

Often, in social situations, I meet up with former colleagues or old hands, or old flames, or whatever you want to call them, and people standing by will say, 'How do you know him?' If he'd been with me the whole time in Belfast I'd often say, 'We used to sleep together!' Because we did: we slept in dormitories together, we ate together, we showered together, we went out on calls together. The camaraderie was unbelievable. We had to look out for one another. You trusted your life to those around you. And they trusted you, that if things went wrong, you would help. So, for example, breathing apparatus was a very important part of the kit. Each breathing apparatus had a personal distress unit on it, and if you were stuck, you activated that. You were looking for your mates to come and get you – that's one example of the camaraderie. There were all sorts of things that were done where you called on your mates to come and help you.

Only once in the ten years or so that I was in the service did I think that I would actually die. That was at Tynan Abbey where two of us were put into a first-floor window because it was thought that there were still staff members in that very large house. As soon as we got into the room and put our breathing sets back on, I knew that the fire was getting out of control. We could feel extreme heat on those parts of our skin that were exposed. There was virtually a stampede for the two of us to get back out of a very small window. In those days we still had some wooden ladders, and we had a thirty-five-foot ladder – an 'Ajax' ladder. The top of this wooden ladder had started to be involved in the fire. So that was a close call. But I have to say, for me, it wasn't life or death too often, that was actually very rare. But on that one occasion I was reliant on my mate, and he was reliant on me. We had to help each other to get out and down the ladder and off to safety.

Keady

Keady sits close to the border and is about seven miles from its larger neighbour, Armagh. It was the scene of a number of serious incidents and the local firefighters were – as was the case in other more rural areas – the first emergency responders to many of those attacks.

Liam Quinn

Within just a few months of joining, Liam attended the immediate aftermath of a bombing outside the Step Inn pub in Keady.

In August 1976, I'd only been in the retained a few months. I heard a bomb explode and I was up to the station even before the siren started to go off. The fire station was up at the monument at the time. I had Ciaran with me – we drove up. All we had at the time was a Land Rover – the L4P – and it carried a crew of four, and the station had a full complement of eight men. So I think everybody turned out to it. The bomb had gone off without warning outside a local pub and when we arrived, there was pandemonium, with everybody running around trying to help. The explosion put out the street lights and you hadn't the lights and all on machines that you have now. We were working basically with flashlamps when we went inside the building. The L4P carried a crew of four and the other men made their own way to the call. At that time you were allowed, although later on they actually stopped that, but at that time they were allowed to grab their gear and run down the street to it.

Well, when we arrived, the outside wall was down, the whole inside was wrecked. We didn't know who was where. The place had been full of customers and there were people running in and out before we got there and it took a long time to make sure it was completely cleared. We were doing our best with what we had. We were just going in, searching everywhere and trying to find out the whole time from the people that was in it who was out, who was in, who was with you and that type of thing. It was difficult and it took time. Maybe about three o'clock in the morning the army catering corps arrived and they started going round the soldiers with coffee. They had coffee in backpacks, plastic cups and all. So they had done the soldiers and next thing they came over to us and asked did anybody want coffee. It was strong and black and no milk, no sugar. It's strange, I still have the taste of that coffee in my mouth, forty-odd years later.

There were a lot of people injured and got out and there were ambulances coming and going. The lady that owned the bar, her and her husband, they had got out. But when things settled down it turned out she had walked out of the bar, bleeding, went into a house across the road and sat down in the chair – and she died in that house across the road before the ambulance ever got to her. She was Betty McDonald. There was a young man killed standing at his own door across the street, he was eighteen, Gerard McGleenan. Some part of the car hit him. The bomb had been left by the Glenanne Gang.

I'd go to things like that, be out all night, and at half five, six o'clock in the morning, I was back at my work at the bakery. You just went on and did it. Although these things are terrible and miserable, it never had too much effect on me personally. You went back into the station and talked about how bad it was and how dirty, but you left it at that and went on and you didn't talk much about it to anybody.

You even had to be careful when you went back to work. Even with ordinary calls, you went back into work an hour later and you might be asked, 'What was the fire? What were you at?' But you always had to be discreet about what you said.

Because of where Keady is, we had to manage on our own most of the time. Newtownhamilton was the first backup for the town, and Armagh was our backup to Middletown, and we were backup to Armagh and Newtownhamilton. Any call we went out to in the L4P, we knew the nearest backup was at least fifteen minutes behind us. We were going out as a group of four men knowing that we had at least fifteen minutes before anyone else arrived.

Although there was a big army and police presence in the town, we wouldn't have had too much bother. Once you were coming out on the blue lights, if the army was in the town, they heard the siren and saw you coming and there wasn't usually a problem. When the station was here and I was coming with the car and there was a patrol in the middle of the town – they would spread out, someone checking here and someone checking the cars down there – I'd have the hazard lights on and would shout to the first fellow, 'I'm going to a fire.' He'd usually stand out in the road and shout at the rest to clear the road and let me through.

As I said, the station had only eight personnel, so things could get tight. There was an incident one night – again we got the call up at the station with the L4P. The fire was up at the monument. I'd seen the fire as I was driving by it. It was a small supermarket a couple of doors down from the monument. We arrived up and next thing somebody shouted in that the paper shop was on fire – that was up Davis Street, and we had only six men all together. Next minute, someone came running shouting that another wee shop up the street was on fire. Three shops in the town on fire at the one time and we had one Land Rover and six men – and the nearest backup was fifteen minutes away.

But we divided up: we had two men going to each call. We set the L4P out the front of the monument and ran one line down the street to the supermarket and one up to the paper shop. The L4P sat in the middle of the road pumping to both of them. The man who owned the shop next door was footing the ladder for me and I was on my own just with that. The other boys, a couple of them were at the drapers shop and a couple of others went to the other shop with fire extinguishers to try to save as much as they could. You could laugh at it now – you had three fires in the town and you didn't know if there was a fourth one going to go up. Was a fifth one going to go up? There was that many going off at the one time. Then we got a Bedford pump ladder, which carried a crew of six and our personnel was increased to twelve.

Sometimes we got calls to other station's areas because they were out – or because we were the backup appliance. One such happened in July 1990. We were sent to the Killylea Road to a bomb explosion. It was a culvert under the road that blew up as a police car went over it. The car went up in the air over the hedge, ten or twelve foot high, and came down the other side into a ditch, roof first. We had to take the bodies out of the car but we couldn't get doors open so it took time. Three policemen were killed and a nun travelling along the road, coming in the opposite direction, died too. You go to an ordinary call and you are craicing and talking to one another, even if there's a fire, but there's nothing serious involved. But at the like of that everybody's standing about, nobody's speaking. It's completely quiet – you'd nearly think the birds were away too.

As a result of the security situation in South Armagh, the army and police regularly moved around by helicopter. These were rarely attacked from the ground, but on rare occasions weapons and rocket-type devices were fired at them when they were near their bases. Liam recalls one such attack that had an unusual start – and finish.

Not everything is awful though – even when you think it's going to be. I was at work one morning – it was maybe about ten o'clock – when the alerter went and I headed down to the station. By then we had got a teleprinter that gave you the address and what you were going to and all. It just said 'Assist Newtownhamilton at Dundalk Street', so we'd go as backup to Newtown. There was no word of what the call was, no word of house fire, or accident, just 'assist Newtown'. We had a couple of new men and they were on the crew out of the six. Again I was the leading firefighter, I was officer in charge, I was driver, I was everything! But these two men, this was maybe their second or third call and another man was only in a couple of months. We got in and booked mobile and coming up the street we heard Newtown booked out to the call on the radio. Their sub officer, PJ Murray, he came on and he booked mobile and he told control he saw the helicopter being hit and saw it coming down in the school field. Knowing the area, he figured out that the school playing fields would have been the backup to the helicopter if anything did happen. They had the landing pad in near the station. So I said to the boys 'You may get ready for this, you don't know what you are going to.' You knew by the way he said it that the helicopter was taking off out of the barracks and he saw it being hit by a mortar or rocket of some sort.

We headed on up to it anyway and there wasn't much talk. I told the crew to check their BA kits – you check all that sort of thing in case you need them. PJ had booked an attendance at the school and was giving the information that the helicopter was on its side in the school playing fields. So we got to it anyway and it's lying there. We got down into the car park and everyone was standing about, there was nothing to do – some smoke coming out of it, but no fire. A couple of officers arrived, and the soldiers were around it with the whole area sealed off. It turned out the helicopter had been taking off out of the station after picking up a patrol to drop them off somewhere, to man the road or whatever, when they were hit by a mortar of some description. The pilot managed to get it to the field. He said himself that even though it was the school holidays, he knew from his experience going in and out that the Newtown children played in the school fields during the holidays. He was just hoping there was no children on the fields when he was going down – but lucky enough there wasn't. When he got down it rolled as he landed. There was maybe eight or ten soldiers in it and one policeman – there used to be a policeman who would go out on patrol with them. The policeman sprained his ankle and that was the only injury in the whole thing. But there was still a chance of it going on fire – it was full of fuel and all that. Then someone said that there were two machine guns mounted on it and it contained live ammunition and they didn't know what way the ammunition had spilled. The helicopter had rolled over so they didn't know what way the ammunition was. So they were afraid and they were trying to get everybody to move back in case it caught fire and started going off. They came up with the bright idea that they needed to park something to block the bullets if they went off. Some of the officers decided that the Keady machine, which was fifteen years of age, was the most expendable, so they parked it down at an angle to block any bullets. We'd been looking for a new pump for a long time so we were kind of hoping the bullets would go off and shoot the side out of it – but it didn't. It turned out a bit of a laugh at the end of the day.

No matter how much you train, you need a bit of good fortune. There was one night, it was our training night and we were up in the square in Keady. It was back in the time of the L4P. Dermot Beattie was the leading firefighter on the Land Rover, and the whole crew was out in the square training. Dermot's sister had a shop and lived next door to it, a small sweet shop, but she had retired and given the use of the shop to two of her nephews, two young fellas just leaving school who were seventeen or eighteen years of age. It is a big supermarket now. She gave them the use of the premises to build it up. But next thing, one of the young fellows came running down to his uncle saying someone was leaving a bomb in the shop. There was an officer in Portadown at that time, Ronnie Bell. He had his time done and hadn't made up his mind if he was retiring or was staying on. He could have stayed on another few years or whatever. While he was making up his mind, they'd sent him out in Portadown, where they were short of officers at the time, and this particular training night he was out with us. Dermot told his nephew to go up to the barracks and tell them about the bomb, so Ronnie said he'd go up with them in case they mightn't believe a young fella they didn't know. He told Dermot to book the crew on so we were standing by.

Next thing the army came and the ATO arrived, closed off the roads, and we were standing by. Everything went on for hours, as it does. Eventually, at maybe eleven o'clock or twelve o'clock, they cleared it. It was a parcel made to look like a bomb – but it was a hoax. So that was all right, and we were starting to make up. After they had changed out of their firefighting gear Dermot took Ronnie up to the street, to show him the shop. About a hundred yards from the shop they walked across the road and there was a car parked along the footpath. Ronnie had his hand on the side of the car as he stepped on to the footpath and the boot lid blew open. Turned out, the bomb in the shop was a hoax, a decoy to draw the police or army in, but there was something like a five- or six-hundred-pound bomb in the boot of the car. As the boys stepped on to the footpath, the detonator on it blew, but the bomb didn't go off. That's how close those two boys came to being blown apart. Ronnie rang the fire brigade HQ the next morning – he had made up his mind what he was doing.

Newry

Newry's location close to the border gives it a strong sense of place. Driving south on the A1, it's the last big town before you leave Northern Ireland – or the first one you arrive at when you're driving north. As the Troubles worsened, the town was increasingly in the firing line. From attacks on commercial property to attacks on the security forces, violence grew to an intense level, and local firefighters carried a considerable weight on their shoulders.

James Fitzpatrick

Served in Newry throughout his firefighting career, first in the auxiliary service and then in the retained.

On the morning the Troubles really started in Newry, we were called out at around six o'clock in the morning. It was the fourth call of the night as far as I can remember – a car was burned. I think that was the first 'internment night'. We arrived at the station, we got the call, we answered the call, but when we got back and were dismissed we weren't allowed home. We had to stay in the station for, I think it was, two days and two nights. We were sleeping on the floor, no beds. We were lying in our uniform. That was the start and we had several calls over the following week. Things were bad.

There were a lot of lives lost and more than you'd even think. There was a bomb explosion in a pub in Newry on Christmas Eve – 1973, I think – in Clarke's on Monaghan Street. It was terrible. There wasn't a lot we could do. We sent a woman who had nasty burns over to the butcher's shop on the opposite side of the street. Back then I wouldn't have been any more than my mid-/late thirties. Even till the present day, if I walked into Clarke's, which is all modernised, I'd lift my legs to stop myself from walking over the bodies, to stop myself walking over something, even though it's all modernised. I do have nightmares. Things have got harder over the years. If I hear the least wee noise at all, I'm alert.

There was another incident, I don't think it had anything to do with the Troubles, but the Troubles made a difference. There was a fire in a shop in Hill Street and two boys lost their lives. They'd broken into the premises and the fire started and we were at it for two days. It actually happened on Friday. We were there Friday, Friday night, Saturday, and then we were relieved and then we were back again on Sunday when we found the two bodies. Now my cousin Barney was never the better of it – he took it to the grave with him. He maintained that there was a third boy because when he was answering the call, coming out on his bike, there'd been a boy running up High Street with his hair on fire.

There were dummies in the window that were melting in the heat. There was a lot of rioting and I think the rioters thought that the dummies were people but that the army and police weren't letting us in to help them and put the fire out. The rioting didn't have any effect on what we were doing. We just pulled out our axes – at that time you had them on your belt – and we kept them in our hands. In later years someone said to me that firemen didn't do this and didn't do that, and I turned round and said, 'Were you at it?'

'No, no, a friend told me about it …'

Says I, 'I was one of the firemen who was at it.'

Even in the middle of all the terrible stuff, there's often a funny side. We got a call that the post office vans were on fire – the post office used to be on Hill Street and part of it opened out on to the Mall where the bus depot is now – and when we arrived four or five vans were burned. There was a crowd in the car park and they started to throw petrol bombs at us. There was a senior officer from Lisburn and a sub officer, and all we could hear was shouting. So the machine pulled out, still connected, the hose trailing after it. The police came and everyone ran up the street and all you could hear were the officers: 'Have you got the keys?'

'I haven't got the keys!'

'Where are the keys?'

This was what was going on – you could hear them trying to find the staff car keys. Anyway, we turned round to move back. The police came across Monaghan Street Bridge and a sergeant came across from the policemen rapping the shields, saying, 'It's all right, we're here, we're here, don't worry about it. We'll control the crowd.' Before we got as far as the bridge that boy passed us in the opposite direction – the crowd was too much for them!

Through it all, though, the general atmosphere in the station was, well ... everybody was just the same as they always were – we were a happy family and looked after one another. That was just basically what it was all about. Not like now, when the retained boys go to the station for their training, then at half nine they're away. In our day we would sit and play cards, you know, hang around for a while. Oh aye, it was a challenge because you didn't know what you were going to. And you never talked about it – when you went back to the station you never said anything about the call. But it all stays with you. Even now, I'm still keen – I'm eighty years of age and I'm still a fireman. If someone fell walking across the road I'd be the first one over, can't help it. Probably in the blood. My grandfather was in the fire brigade in the 1900s. He died in 1947 and his remains were carried down on top of the old fire engine. His son, Barney Junior – my uncle – and Barney Junior's son, Bernie, were in the fire brigade. And then there was his cousin, my grandfather's brother's son. I was the fifth member of the family to be in it and the last one. Last one in and the last one out!

I could kick myself now for my own stupidity that I left the service. My wife died, she was only forty-two and I had four boys so I had to make a choice and the choice was the family. She'd been unwell for six or seven years. Somebody mentioned to her one time, 'How come you have four boys and no girls?' Do you know what her answer was? 'Seamus was running to too many fires.' She had a sense of humour, God rest her.

Lurgan

In the past, Lurgan had its traditional industries – linen, engineering and the like – and at the start of the Troubles, it would not have been an obvious target. However, for many reasons, the town and its hinterland was on the receiving end of numerous attacks and sectarian violence. The commercial centre took a real pasting on a number of occasions and both rioting and attacks on the security forces were routine. Although the number of incidents had declined by the mid–nineties, they increased again with the civil unrest that resulted from the Drumcree dispute. This violence was widespread and at a level of intensity not seen since the height of the Troubles.

Jim Crozier
Writes of his experiences of firefighting in the town.
At 7 p.m. on Tuesday 6 December 1969, I reported for duty at Lurgan Fire Station to commence training as a retained firefighter. This was the start of a career that was to last for the next thirty-six years. Little did I know at that time that I and the rest of the men I served with would be called upon to carry out tasks that went far beyond the normal everyday firefighting duties we might have anticipated, as Northern Ireland entered the Troubles. Section Leader Gerald Cassells was the officer in charge of the Lurgan section. Gerry, as he was known, led the section through some of the worst incidents we were called upon to attend. He was a man highly

respected by all who knew him, someone who never asked anyone to do something he couldn't do himself. He also taught me everything I know about firefighting.

In 1969 Lurgan Station attended fewer than a hundred calls-outs; by the mid-1980s that total had risen to over a thousand calls per year. This rapid rise required many sacrifices, not only from the personnel involved but also from their families, who, when their men answered a call, were left behind not knowing if they would return safely. Lurgan, like other towns, suffered greatly as a result of terrorist attacks and we attended the majority of those incidents. We also attended incidents across Northern Ireland when called upon. I remember many of these, but the following have stayed particularly in my memory.

On 24 November 1971 at around 6.30 p.m. terrorists planted a bomb in Fisher's shop. When the siren sounded I responded to the station. I lived close to William Street at the time. Two appliances, with Section Leader Cassells in charge, responded to William Street to find the building was on fire. A bomb disposal officer who had been called to deal with the device had entered the building and a few minutes later the device detonated. This was now a fire and rescue situation and over the coming hours the crews worked tirelessly in very dangerous conditions to extinguish the fire and find that officer. At one point during operations a gas cylinder exploded, sending a ball of fire towards us, but luckily none of us were injured. Eventually we recovered the body of Warrant Officer Colin Davies close to the front of the shop. We all returned to station with heavy hearts that night. Unlike today there was no counselling or any other kind of support following this type of incident and we had to deal with it as best we could. Fisher's was just the first of many such incidents we would be called to in the years ahead.

It was a beautiful Sunday evening, 18 June 1972, when we received a call to Cranny Lane, Bleary. Section Leader

Cassells was given an instruction by controls to respond without using blue lights or air horns, which seemed strange. On arrival we found police, army and ambulance personnel in attendance at a bungalow, which had been virtually demolished in an explosion. Army personnel had been searching the bungalow following a tip-off, but the search revealed nothing. The same team were sent in again to search more thoroughly and, this time, triggered a booby-trap bomb, causing an explosion which badly injured and trapped a number of them. Police officers who were outside the building were also injured and were being treated by ambulance crews. Using the limited resources we had then – mainly axes, crowbars, jacks and brute force – we set to work aided by army personnel in an effort to extract three casualties. Two were trapped under part of the collapsed roof and the third was in the rubble. These rescues took some time, but we eventually extracted the men and they were then attended to by medical personnel. Sadly, despite all our efforts, they did not survive their injuries: Arthur McMillan, Ian Mutch and Colin Leslie died at the scene.

In addition to the bomb, another weapon of choice for the terrorists was the incendiary device. Hard to detect, these caused untold damage in properties across the country. Lurgan came under attack from these devices on a number of occasions, but due to the fires often, fortuitously, being detected quickly, we were able to extinguish them before shops were seriously damaged. However, in the early hours of Sunday 18 August 1974, that all changed when a number of properties were targeted and, as a result, very seriously damaged in concentrated incendiary device attacks on the town centre. The first call, to the Tweed Shop in Market Street, was received at 12.30 a.m. On arrival we were met with flames roaring out through the front windows and licking up the front of the building. Jets were deployed and Firefighter Alvin McNally and I donned breathing apparatus and proceeded to tackle the fire. We fought our way into the shop, extinguishing the fire as we went. It was a very long building and it took a lot of effort to drag a fully-charged hose line to the back of it. Happy that we had extinguished the fire but conscious that there might be other devices around that had not ignited, we withdrew. To our surprise there were now only two other firefighters outside. Another call had been received to Miss O'Neill's drapers shop in High Street and Section Leader Cassells had responded to deal with this fire. He had also called for more appliances to be sent into Lurgan. As I took my BA set off, I felt a hand on my shoulder and a civilian alerted me to a fire in Corkin's furniture shop. I looked back up Market Street to see smoke and flames coming out of the front of the building. I immediately radioed our control room for more appliances and set off in our third appliance, with firefighters McNally and McNicholl, to tackle this fire. We were joined by Station Officer Victor Spence, who had been at the second incident. Although few in number, we got to work and I deployed Firefighter McNicholl with a jet to the front of the building. Almost immediately he slipped on broken glass and cut his wrist. Firefighter McNally took his place and as Firefighter McNicholl was being led away to be treated I heard a shout – firefighter McNally had also fallen and been cut! Now there was only the station officer and myself left standing.

However, a few minutes later, backup crews arrived from Portadown and were deployed straightaway. The building to the left of the fire comprised a ground floor shoe shop with a Chinese restaurant above. The OIC of the Portadown crews was instructed to enter these premises and put stopper jets in place. The front door was promptly broken down and he entered the property. As he made his way up the stairs leading to the Chinese, he was met by a man carrying a large meat cleaver – who then chased him into the street. Police officers intervened and relieved him of his weapon. He'd had no idea the building next door was on fire and had only woken up when the door was broken down. We had a laugh about it afterwards – but it could have had a bad outcome. Seven properties were severely damaged and costs were estimated at over one million pounds. Thirteen fire crews responded to Lurgan that night in order to bring these fires under control.

In the early hours, as dawn broke, another fire broke out in the Tweed Shop after undiscovered incendiary devices exploded at the very back of the shop, resulting in the fire travelling up through two more floors. When I look back, we made the right decision to get out of there when we did. Crews stayed on duty long into Sunday night before all the fires were totally extinguished. Then, on Monday morning our crews were called to the Woolworths store in High Street when further incendiary devices were discovered. Fortunately this time the damage was minimal.

On another occasion, we received a call to Glendinnings factory on Lake Street and upon arrival were faced with a hostile crowd. As there was no apparent sign of fire, the section leader ordered the crew to stay on the appliance and he went into the factory to investigate. At this point our second appliance pulled up behind us. After about two minutes the section leader returned and, as he opened the appliance door, the stoning started. He was struck on the side of his helmet by a brick. It almost brought him to his knees but he recovered, mounted the appliance and ordered the driver to get us out of there. Off we went, thinking the second appliance was behind us. Some distance along the road we realised it wasn't and then came a radio message that the driver, Firefighter McShane, was injured, having been blinded by glass when a brick shattered the side window as he pulled away. He was now only able to operate the foot pedals of the appliance and the officer in charge was steering as they made their way slowly to safety. This injury resulted in him being off for many months before being able to return to duty. The fire call was a hoax designed to draw us into the area.

While Firefighter McShane was able to return to duty, this wasn't always the case for injured firefighters. Whilst attending a fire at a single-storey building on the Ardowen estate in Craigavon, it became necessary to increase the water supply to the appliances. When Firefighter George Gardiner went around a corner in order to find another fire hydrant he was so badly assaulted that he was forced to retire from the service. Shortly after this incident we attended a house fire in the same estate, which resulted in persons having to be rescued and taken to hospital. Some days later our station officer returned to enquire about these people. As he sat talking to the lady involved, a man walked in and, without identifying himself, said he believed we were having trouble in this area – to which the station officer replied, 'Yes, we are.'

'You won't have any more trouble here,' came the reply. With that he turned and walked out. From that day the attacks on us in the area stopped.

As the number of terrorist incidents increased, on many occasions we were called to other towns, such as Portadown, Banbridge, Armagh, Lisburn, Markethill and Newry, to assist their crews. It was while dealing with a row of houses on fire in Watson Street, Portadown, that I truly felt our lives were in danger. As we got to work tackling the fire, a man approached the pump operator and kicked the hose from his hand as he was about to connect it to the appliance. A short scuffle ensued and he was pushed away. He turned back, pointed a finger at us and said, 'There's a hood for every one of you on that machine.' Then off he went into the darkness. We carried on firefighting, but while I was up a ladder I looked around and saw him returning, his jacket open and a gun clearly visible. It was time to go … He stood watching as we shut down the water supply, disconnected the equipment and left the area.

Thankfully most people welcomed us as they were only too glad of our help. One such person was Lurgan Salvation

Army Captain John Brook-Smith. He formed a close bond with us and would turn up in his car at all times of the night and day and in all weathers with tea urns and food for us as we went about our duties. Sometimes he spent as much time on a fire ground as we did and he deserves to be remembered for his compassion and support.

I was promoted to the rank of leading firefighter in 1974 and eventually, after Sub Officer Cassells retired, I was appointed as sub officer in charge in 1981. During my time in charge I was called upon to attend – with our emergency service unit – two incidents well outside our station's area. The first was the Ballygawley bus bombing. The second was the Omagh bombing. Much has been said and written about both – suffice to say, they left a lasting impression on all the personnel who attended. Despite the challenges the job brought, I was proud to be a part of and to eventually lead the personnel of the Lurgan Section who faithfully served all sides of the community. I left the brigade in February 2006 having served for just over thirty-six years.

Crossmaglen

Crossmaglen Fire Station in South Armagh can certainly be seen as far from typical, either in comparison to other local stations, or to any in the rest of the United Kingdom. As the Troubles escalated, Crossmaglen's location and demographic put it well and truly on the 'front line'. Sitting almost on the border with the Republic of Ireland, it became a significant base for the British Army and the RUC – with all the attendant challenges for the locals and for the security forces.

Until the late seventies Crossmaglen had no 'proper' fire station – it relied entirely on a dedicated group of local volunteers who organised and trained themselves and used a basic array of firefighting equipment that they took to fires on a trailer. As well as the challenge of facing serious incidents when help is some distance away, they had no fire engine, no modern firefighting kit, no rescue equipment and no breathing apparatus.

The volunteers' struggle to get recognition and support from the Northern Ireland Fire Brigade was protracted, but eventually successful, and the town finally got the service the volunteers had worked so hard for.

Peter Clarke

Joined the volunteers' fire station in Crossmaglen in 1972.

In all my time, the worst thing for me was the explosion in Silverbridge in 1975. Boys attacked Donnelly's bar – shot up the place and put a bomb in. We heard that they shouted 'Happy Christmas' or something before driving off. We went to it and there were bodies cut near in half everywhere, bits here and bits there. It was an awful mess and the two of us were sick, we threw our guts up. I'd never seen anything like it. The smell of burning flesh, it was unreal. That was the worst thing. I had nightmares about that. I would waken up, shouting in my sleep many's a time – Silverbridge was the worst one for that. With me working in Cumiskys, I delivered stuff to Donnelly's, and I knew a lot of the men. It took me a long time to get over that. It sickened me.

Being a fireman in the town during the Troubles was difficult enough. We got a hard time from the soldiers often enough: they literally thought every man in Crossmaglen was lying and they seemed to run round like John Wayne. We had no bleepers at that time and you had to run to a fire and the soldiers would hold you back. You had to show your pass. Before we got a fire engine, we had a trailer and the soldiers assumed it was something else on the trailer, but you could see it was a hose, an old garden hose that we had. They would put you out and search you, the house could be burnt by the time you got to it and that happened several times.

Even talking now it seems like a distant memory, that it never happened. I have grandchildren that never heard of it, boys at nineteen, and they don't understand and have never known what trouble is. Jesus, I wouldn't like them coming up through that. How did we come up through it? What could you do? You had to go on. People thought it was to do with religion – it was nothing to do with religion; it was to do with the British Army. There's the Protestant church there, and the Catholic church just down the road. We always drank together in the pub – it was nothing to do with Protestant and Catholic, it was just the British Army going in, all right. Sure we used to talk to them when they first came to Crossmaglen, they were in the pub drinking. But then there was two policemen blown up near Lissaraw. I knew them well – Sam Donaldson and Robert Millar, they were two lovely lads. We all cried ourselves – it was fucking terrible. It was an awful time to die. Things changed. We all remember Sergeant Reid that run the youth club in Crossmaglen and we wouldn't have had a youth club only for him. People don't realise, they think it was only ever the one way.

For years we were a volunteer station and we had to do the job with near enough nothing. One road accident I was at, there were two girls trapped in the back and we couldn't open the doors, we had no equipment at all and they were screaming, 'Help! Take me out.' I said, 'I can't – I can't touch, I can't go near, I have to wait until the ambulance comes. I could do more harm getting you out of the car.' The boy, the driver, his bone had come through his knees and they were screaming at me; they were shouting away. We could do nothing, we were standing listening to them crying.

We thought we were never going to get a proper fire engine. Fortunately we had a very determined local man called Gene Donaghy who wanted to make things better. Gene was a businessman in Crossmaglen and had a brilliant sense of community. He and a few other businessmen got together to form a local fire service because people's homes and businesses were being burnt to the ground before Newtownhamilton fire brigade got there. He had a garage with a shed down the back of a big yard and he let us use this to store the trailer and the few bits of kit we had. The way we thought was – and this is the truth, right or wrong – we are nationalists and they are not going to give us anything. Gene Donaghy, he fought hard and they still wouldn't give him one. But he wouldn't give up and continued to fight passionately for Crossmaglen fire brigade to be recognised. It was his pride and joy to see it becoming a proper retained crew with its own dedicated fire station. Gene was a wonderful man who did his best for his community.

One day we got a call out to the school, me and Peter McCallister. We went into the science room and we only saw a wee bit of the fire. Peter McAllister told me to get the first aid hose – he was the leading fireman – and we spread the whole thing round. We stopped it spreading and saved the school – and that was all right – but we had no breathing apparatus then and the fumes after that, it left us in the hospital. I was in for a week. It affected my kidneys, I had the bag, I couldn't pee for a fortnight. Then, one of the local full-time officers who covered South Armagh came down. To tell you the truth, I never liked him, because he was a sour git. He came in and he ate the head off us – 'What the hell were you doing?'

We said, 'We were trying to put the fire out.'

He says, 'That wasn't what you were supposed to do, you wee fuckers.'

He ate the head off us and said we were going to get him into trouble.

I said, 'How are you going to get into trouble? You weren't there.' Some good came out of it, though – we got a fireman's wage for twelve months, that was the compensation we got, and that was quite a bit of money at that time. Gene played on it – he got into the *Armagh Observer* and the Newry paper and it was all over the page: 'Two Cross men injured in fire blast'. It blew it up, so there was a big meeting. I don't know who was at it but Gene could argue and there was a real row. 'This is blatantly a sectarian thing,' he says. 'I thought this was for everybody but we seem to get nothing here. I nearly lost two men.' Nobody wanted to hear that. Things got better after that and now we're as well kitted-out as any station – but a lot of things had to happen to get this and Gene fought hard for us.

For me it was a big thing to be a fireman. I was born delicate, only a pound or two in weight. My twin was heavier but he died when he was three months and they were all waiting for me to die. I was born with my leg twisted round and I never really was at school much – I never got much education until I was fourteen. I was only at school a year and a half when I left it. I was fifteen when I left and I couldn't count to a hundred. I was in Cumiskys and over the years Jack Cumisky came to me and taught me how to read the tape and my wife taught me to read every Sunday with the paper. I could hardly spell my name when I met her but I got on rightly. I started learning how to weld and then started my own business working at night, building sheds, making gates. I literally knew nothing and I said to Gene that I'd not be fit to be a fireman but he stuck by me. He says, 'Peter, I'll teach you, don't worry about the writing or the book work.' Years later he says, 'Didn't I tell you you'd be a fireman? You said you wouldn't be – but you are.' And he was right.

The aftermath of the bomb attack on the Killyhevlin Hotel, Enniskillen, 1996.
(Stefan Rousseau/PA Images)

THE SOUTH-WEST

Belleek

The Irish border runs from near Derry/Londonderry in the north-west to close to Newry in the south-east. It is not like the straight lines of state borders in the USA or the 'natural' lines of other borders that closely follow geographical features, rather it is more higgledy-piggledy in nature. The politics of partition in 1920/21 created a border that zigzagged across the land and produced some interesting anomalies. The practical outworking of this meant that towns like Belleek in the extreme west of County Fermanagh had to live with these quirks.

When the Fire Authority decided that the time was right for Belleek to get its first fire station in 1975, they initially rented an old garage workshop on the Enniskillen Road. As Enniskillen, like Belleek, is in Northern Ireland, this sounds fairly unremarkable. However, dealing with a fire in the village of Belleek actually involved the local firefighters crossing the border into the Republic of Ireland and then crossing into a different part of Northern Ireland to get to the station and get the fire engine – then doing the reverse to get to the fire – and then doing the reverse of all of that again to get home. Not a typical fire brigade response. While this might have been merely annoying and inconvenient in any normal circumstance, the Troubles gave it a distinct edge, and every time the local retained firefighters responded to the station they were acutely aware of the potential to be caught in an attack on or near those crossing points.

Joe O'Loughlin
Owned a petrol station on the main street in Belleek and was one of the first volunteer firefighters in the town. Along with those volunteer colleagues, he was in the first group of retained firefighters formally brought into the Northern Ireland Fire Brigade when it established the station in 1975. He describes his earliest days of firefighting.

I'm not 100 per cent sure, but I think it was around the time we joined the European Union that it became compulsory to have a fire service within a fifteen-minute call-out of a town and so we started to get things here. In the early days, equipment was kept in a wooden locker in the local police station. All we had was a standpipe, bar and key, three lengths of hose and a branch. We would take the equipment out of the locker, throw it into the boot of the car and go wherever. If a call came in, we had no proper system – telephones weren't very common, never mind mobile phones – but we somehow got the word out and responded and did our best with what we had.

There was a hotel down at the bottom of the street and they were bombed numerous times. A bomb had been left this day and the police were informed. The local doctor, Dr Finn, had a phone and he came across to where I lived at the top of the village and we went across the fields to the police barracks, a dangerous thing to do because if the army saw you crossing the fields they would have shot you. Anyway, we got to the hotel and sheltered behind a wall until the bomb went off. Then we ran round and got our equipment connected up and were able to prevent the hotel from being seriously damaged by fire. Had we not prevented the fire, the whole villa would have been burned. Enniskillen was our backup and they were a good thirty to forty minutes away. The Enniskillen guys were very efficient – we got on well with them – but it was a long wait.

Noel Brown then became our district officer and he arrived in that job as we were looking for more kit, more training and support. We'd been tackling it with just a few lengths of hose and a branch. So I suppose we proved we were deserving and it was set up. Then you needed the first training in the barracks and Noel Brown showed us how to operate hydrants properly and all that sort of thing. We eventually got a fire engine – an L4P – in the late seventies, I think it was. George Cathcart, a local councillor, worked hard to get us proper resources. He had a big influence in getting a permanent station built here. He knew what we were like and he held me in high esteem. We eventually got a new modern station.

Because of where we are and the border, things were always a bit different for us. There was an occasion when a transport bus was hijacked and set on fire just up at the bridge – the bridge on the border we had to cross to go and get the fire engine – so we couldn't go to the fire station that way. We had to go and then come back the circular route and when we started to deal with it some boys on the other side of the border started to shout at us, told us to fuck off, so we felt a little bit intimidated. Later I met the inspector of the Garda, and I told him we weren't happy about this and that he should do something about it. I think even these guys, they probably understood that we were neutral, you know, and some of them were natives of the area, who had gone across the border. So these guys were made aware that we were neutral and when we went out to a call there was a respect for that. But it wasn't perfect.

Like all retained stations, Belleek had a weekly training night. Within the service this is called a 'drill night' and a full-time officer will regularly come to the station to supervise the training and help sort the routine paperwork. Drill night is a vital part of keeping station personnel skills high and also helps build team spirit, but Northern Ireland's particular situation could make for unusual training.

There was one occasion in the old fire station when we were drilling. We had one of the senior bosses down from Derry and after he left the next thing the door bust open and armed men came in, one of them with a big revolver in his hand. One of our members used to do a bit of cleaning work at the police station and they took him out, took him across the border, put a bomb in his car and told him to drive it to the station. We were tied up; we were told to lie down. You didn't get a chance to see anything, you know – you were told to lie down and keep your head down. We thought we were going to get a bullet in the head. But obviously some of the guys in that raiding team knew us personally and some of us they didn't tie too tight, so we were able to get the rope off ourselves later. The bomb went off but nobody was hurt. When they left they told us to stay put but we managed to untie ourselves. It was a terrifying experience. I wrote into headquarters pointing out that Percy, one of our local officers, had shown great leadership and courage even though he'd been tied up. He got a commendation, which he deserved for that.

Being local meant having local knowledge and while in most places that was usually more about which road to use to get to a fire or where the nearest hydrant was, in Belleek other local knowledge could prove handy.

There was an odd one in the latter stages of the Troubles – one of the last incidents – quite close to where I lived. Somebody told the local police there was a bomb in a clump of bushes and I knew that the army patrols where I lived used to walk across this lane and out on patrol away to a house where that clump of bushes was.

I was working at the time in my garage and I was heading home for my dinner. The local sergeant, I stopped with him and I said, 'The whole area on this side of town is evacuated, school and all, but there's no need to evacuate – that bomb's in a clump of bushes half a mile away.' My farm crossed the border, you see, and the guy that I had rented some of the land to, he said, 'I was down this evening and there was a command wire from the forest right to this clump of bushes.' So I phoned the Garda and let them know and they said they'd send someone out. I kept an eye out and there was no sign of anybody coming and eventually I phoned the Garda again, and I said, 'They must be great guys you have – experts in keeping hidden. I'm fed up with this bloody thing. Will you catch a hold and sort it?'

It so happened I had to go and visit family in Enniskillen and, on the way back, the army stopped me at the end of the lane. I told them who I was and they let me go down. We came then to the other house and this officer-type was there and he had all his equipment set up to deal with it. I said, 'You know that bomb you are dealing with is two hundred yards inside the border of the Republic and if you go on ahead you will cause an international incident.' He took off his cap and took out a map and I went over and told the sergeant that the bomb was over the border and that he would have a serious problem if he dealt with it. I said to the sergeant that I had the land maps over in the village, and that I would go up and would be able to show them exactly where the border was. So they then had to withdraw from the whole thing and let the Irish Army deal with it. But it is one of the few occasions where a British Army officer apologised to me, saying he was wrong and I was right. Being in the fire brigade you needed to know the place well. You see incompetent members of the IRA had read the map wrong and they put it in the wrong clump of bushes. The Garda sergeant was fucking annoyed – because now he had to get the Irish bomb squad from Dublin.

There is an old Irish saying that 'humour is the safety valve of the nation' and if you think back to the sorry time in Northern Ireland, going through the whole Troubles, if it wasn't for the fact we had a sense of humour we would never have survived it.

Belleek station and its personnel had a considerable interest in the bigger, wider world of firefighting and actively looked to make connections with fellow firefighters outside of Northern Ireland. Sometimes our ways of doing things seemed a little unconventional to these 'outsiders'.

We liked the craic and I'd say we were probably the only unit anywhere in the country, north or south, that had an exchange partnership with a foreign fire brigade. We linked with these folks in Germany. When we met them we talked about the job, but not to any great extent – it was more like a social thing. We would have stayed with the family over there and then hosted them when they came over here. When I went over first I got on very well with the young lads; they would sit and chat with me. They were only about eighteen or twenty. They were asking me how I came to be chosen as a 'leader' of the fire brigade. I said when we were established we were all equal and the bosses couldn't decide who they would appoint to be in charge of the station. They decided the only way they could solve this problem was to measure everyone's feet and I had the biggest feet – so because of that I was given the post!

Enniskillen

Located in the beautiful Fermanagh lakelands, Enniskillen has a long and interesting history. Very much the county town, it has been a vibrant and thriving place for many years. Tourism plays a significant part in the local economy and even at the height of the Troubles, fishing drew visitors in. The retained station in the town was busy before the Troubles and – until some new stations were opened in the county and in nearby parts of Tyrone – its crews went to incidents significant distances away. They also regularly crossed into the Republic of Ireland to back up local firefighters there. Into this near-idyllic world came the Troubles and the marks that have been left by that period are deep.

Francie Gilleece
Joined the retained service in Enniskillen in 1972 and remembers some of his earliest fire calls.
My first call was to a hotel in Bellanaleck. A man went in

with a suitcase and said he was down to fish, as you would in Fermanagh. He got his room and spent a bit of time in it, then came down with his rod. 'I'm away for a bit of fishing,' he said. 'Back in a couple of hours.' The man who owned the hotel thought there was something not quite right, so he went up to the room and the suitcase was chained to the leg of the bed. It went off and blew the hotel to bits. The hotel would have been half a mile from the lake and there was no other water nearby. Ernie Elliott, God love him, one of the best of the auld hands, set up a pump down at the lake and he did a deep lift there and connected the hoses. He climbed on to the roof of the fire engine and as he moved along he dropped the lengths of hose on the ground – he got them spaced perfect every time.

Someone went into the Carlton Hotel in Belleek one evening and set a bomb on the counter. But some of the smart boys who worked there lifted it and carried it out into the street. Twenty minutes or so later it went off and there was a big blaze but no damage. About a week later, the same boy came back, set one down on the counter and says, 'You'll not lift that one,' and away he ran. He'd just got round the corner when it went off. We were out at that and it was a fierce blaze – burning from end to end. We were there and so was a policeman from Belleek, Paddy Doherty. The police would have ridden the fire engine the odd time with us because it was safer. Paddy was standing just on the corner of Cleary's pub – there's a big fort just across the river – when a bullet went straight between his legs and through the pole of the signpost behind him. You could actually look through the hole and see where the boy fired it from. Paddy was lucky that day. Meanwhile we just carried on firefighting. It was a different world.

One day we got a call to Casey's Hotel in Garrison. It's about six miles out the road. It was burning well – the whole roof was on fire. There was a police scenes of crime officer, the one boy who was always with us, Big Alan, who was six

85

foot five. We were all mates. We saved the hotel – the fire was probably caused by an incendiary in the roof. Crews from Belleek and from Manorhamilton over the border would have been with us. Big Alan did his bit, and we did our bit, and Mrs Casey, God love her, said, 'Yous'll have a drink, boys?' And to be sociable – what's one to do? So she said, 'What are you having?' Big Alan said, 'I'll have a Bush,' and she set down half a bottle. I wasn't drinking at the time and Jim Monaghan was driving, so he wasn't drinking. Alan had plenty to drink, though, so I ended up driving the CID car from Garrison to the gates of Enniskillen police station. He knew we would look after him.

So in those days, the local police knew us. We'd be out at an incident and we'd get a call from control asking if the police should attend. We got a call one frosty night to the Mountview Hotel in Derrylin. They had poured drums of petrol over the floor of the hotel, and lit it, and she was going fairly good. I went down the street to set up the hydrant and there was a man, one of the Provos, legging it over the wall. And he said, 'Just watch the road now – it's slippy.' So I set up the hydrant and got it turned on. Then someone said to me, 'The boys are lining the hedge there.' 'Jesus,' I thought, and the sub got on the radio quick to tell the police not to come. A good while later, as the council officer, I went out on a dog complaint one day. There was someone complaining about a neighbour, so I thought I'd go up and have a word with him. I knocked the door and explained who I was and what I was about. He made me a cup of tea and told me his side of the story.

I said, 'Well, I'll see what I can do,' and he said, 'Oh, I know you will.' I said, 'Why? How do you know me?' He said, 'Do you remember that night in Derrylin? Do you remember the boy going over the wall? That was me.' Now whether it was him or not, I don't know – it probably was. It was good of him or whoever it was to think of my welfare and warn me about the slippy road.

Being the licensing officer for the council, I was in all the local hotels. In the big hotel in Lisnaskea the exit door at the back was inward opening and it should have been outward opening. I had a great running battle with the owners, who I would have been very friendly with, because I didn't like the door being inward opening. But the police came back to me and said that they'd prefer them not to change the door because if the hotel was going to be attacked, they'd come in from the back and if the door was outward opening, they wouldn't be able to slam it in the attacker's face. I debated it with the boss anyway and he decided to let it run for a while as it was.

One Saturday night, they attacked the hotel. Four people came in through the front door from the main street, each with a five-gallon drum of petrol. They counted the incendiary devices going off – one, two, three, four, and you can imagine how well she was burning after those going off. Lisnaskea's crew was there, and we arrived, and I think there must have been fishermen or visitors staying. I was tasked – together with one of the other firemen, John – to go in with the breathing apparatus and search all the rooms to make sure there was no one in them. It was pitch dark and we were making our way along the corridor – you felt this and it was a hat stand; and you felt this, and it was a chair; and I felt this and – 'What the fuck's that?' I said, 'John, hold on a minute,' and I lifted it and I shook it and it splashed. I set it down nice and gently and we ran like blazes down the stairs.

We met the officer coming up the stairs and he said, 'What's wrong?' and I said, 'There's another bomb up there,' and he said, 'There's not – they counted four in and four went off,' and I said, 'No, there's another one.' So we were out anyway and the ammunition technical officer was there, and I says to him, 'When you get it defused, my fingerprints are going to be on it – but I didn't plant it.' They thought it might have come in the back door. So that's how I got the door outward opening – when they rebuilt the hotel and the door went back in, it was outward opening. You can achieve anything if you put your mind to it!

When the siren lifted and a crew responded to the station, the control room told them what they were going to and where it was. Usually this information was accurate and there were no surprises but sometimes, although things might have appeared routine, they were very far from it and normal procedures turned out to be inadequate to the task.

We got a call once to a hayshed in Belcoo, just by the chapel. And the owner of the hayshed owned this pub just over the road. We arrived and started to fight the hayshed and next thing control said, 'Withdraw – we've received threats in relation to you. There are people watching you and ringing us and saying what will happen.' The hayshed was going well and it was going to burn the whole street and I thought, just give us ten minutes and we'll have this under control. The police station was just across the street, about fifty yards away, and the police were starting to get very nervous because obviously they were being fed what we were hearing – the fire brigade was passing it to them. One of the boys was busting for a pee and went round the back of the hayshed but the police, seeing something at the back of the hayshed, fired a flare right over his head and the whole country could see him! It was dark so the whole area was lit up.

A senior officer arrived in his car and said, 'Yous haven't withdrawn – they were advising you to withdraw.'

And I said, 'I know, but if we'd withdrawn it would have burned all that.'

He looked at it and says, 'Well, what do you think?'

'Well, if they were going to open fire on us, they'd have done it before now,' I says.

He says, 'I tell you what I'm doing – I'm getting the hell out of here.'

But we put out the hayshed and went into the pub. We had a free hour and then went home.

You never quite knew what was going to happen. This particular evening was wild frosty – it would have damaged a brass monkey – and we got a call to a wooden custom hut and she was going well. George Elliott was the sub then and he says, 'Let's put her out, boys.' So we started running out the hoses. Then a man – he must have been about six foot five or six foot six – untangled himself out of a wee green minivan. He came struggling over to us and said, 'Boys, go home.' There was no please about it. And I said, 'Who are you?' and he says, 'I'm SAS.'

I live in Enniskillen and I was at home one day when there was some unmerciful explosion. It was that loud that a boy with a chainsaw cutting trees beside me heard it. But nothing happened until about an hour later, when the alerters went and it was a call to a soldier trapped under a Land Rover between Kinawley and Derrylin, about twelve miles away. He was a Royal Marine – they took the doors off the Land Rovers, it was like their signature – and they were coming down towards Kinawley when this massive bomb went off. It blew a tunnel or a trench all up the side of the road about a hundred yards long and five foot deep. The Land Rover went up into the air and landed back down on your man's ankle. Leading Fireman Ken and I worked as two. Ken was digging in from the road and I got into the big trench. Your man was lying with one foot in the drain and one under the Land Rover. I started to dig and hit a stone, and I says to Ken, 'Stand back – I'll hit it a good rap with the crowbar,' and I pulled it back and hit your man right up in the privates. And he says, in his English accent, 'Awwww, my balls, mate!' But we got the stone out and got him free and, just like that, we looked around and he had gone. He'd run up the trench and across the road, jumped the hedge and into the helicopter. The following night the old general came into the fire station and told us he had a broken ankle. He'd done well to run off and jump the hedge.

The L4P was a specially designed fire engine based on a Land Rover chassis that was intended for use by firefighters in rural areas. It carried a limited amount of water and equipment but it had some off-road capabilities.

The L4P was a good idea that didn't quite work. They were a danger to drive, even with the hundred gallons on them. I remember L/F Ken saying that if you were turned out first with her, you'd nothing with you. By the time you filled the hoses, she was empty. We were always waiting for the next crew. They had accident equipment on her, but it would take you forever to get there, especially if you hit a hill.

There was a republican who lived not that far from Enniskillen. He'd had an accident on the farm in Garvary. He was on the tractor in the field and the tractor overturned and landed on him. In those days we'd quite a few tractors that would tumble over and fall on to the driver. There were no cages, no roll bars, so we used to lift the tractors off and then take the poor unfortunate person out from underneath. That was that. In those days they turned out the Land Rover to that sort of thing. Now, the L4P wouldn't have pulled the drawers off a prostitute – she was terrible – and Garvary is a big hill. I was driving the L4P and George was the sub officer.

A good while after that call I was out doing something at Garvary, council work. And this boy says to me, 'That George boy's a quare fucker.' And he says, 'That night of the accident, that Land Rover drove very slow up Garvary,' inferring that we'd deliberately taken our time and that it was because we knew who the farmer was – and George was a Prod. And I said, 'It wasn't him driving – it was me!'

Firefighters responded to any incident to which they were called and one of the defining characteristics of the service during the Troubles was that they could be trying to save the life of a paramilitary one day and military personnel the next. It was essential that personal political views were left at the station door and that help was offered without 'fear or favour'.

One day a reasonably big bomb went off in the town and we were tasked out to it. A car had blown up between the back of the British Legion and the fence at Lakeland Forum [the local leisure centre]. Some soldiers had been at a fishing competition and, when they had got into their car, a booby trap went off. L/F Ken and I were working as a pair and there was this boy lying, not breathing, on the ground. We got the resuscitation oxygen set on him and got him breathing, and the next thing this voice says, 'You can take it off now, boys: he's dead.' It was the doctor, and he was standing watching us do it. He'd wanted to see how we do it, let us do it anyway. Ken and me started to put the soldiers into the back of the ambulance – we put one soldier in and put three legs with him. That's my recollection of it. We all did what we could and there was a fireman there who got a bravery award for looking after them. A number of years later he took his own life. Very sad.

We used to play darts competitions on Saturday afternoons at McCartney's Bar. Raymond McCartney would have been very much a fireman's man – nothing to do with the fire brigade at all but very much a fireman's man. We were playing pool one Saturday afternoon in McCartney's when the siren went off. We went out – a young lad had been killed about a mile outside the town – and then we came back and started arguing about what the score was. Someone says, 'What were you at?' and we replied, 'We were at an accident.'

'Was anyone hurt?'

'Aye, there was a fella killed,' and there we were playing pool after it. But that's the way you dealt with these things. We never got any counselling and we really should have done. I'd go so far as to say that we still should do, without a shadow of a doubt. I can't look at an accident or a crash on the television or anything like that. I can't even read in the paper about it. And that's just myself – and I'm twenty years out of it.

It's not Troubles-related – but I got a laugh this day. As we went out to a chimney fire, the other pump got turned out to a high school – the roof was on fire. When we made ourselves available they turned us out to the high school too. Now you couldn't get down the sides of the high school – you had to go up on to a flat roof and go down the back of it. Ken Ramsey had gone on to the flat roof and disappeared. I arrived and I knew I was going to have to go up on to the roof. My brother-in-law Seamus was in the fire brigade too and he followed me up to the roof. It was an odd layout and very slippy, and Seamus fell off and broke his femur. He fell about ten or twelve foot and landed on uneven ground. One of the crew, Frankie Elliott, was a real gentleman and big in the Salvation Army and there was Seamus shouting, 'Oh my fucking leg! Oh my fucking leg!' He looked up and saw Frankie there and said, 'Oh, sorry, Frankie, I didn't mean to say that.'

'It's all right, Seamus, it's all right,' says Frankie and after a slight pause Seamus starts again, 'Oh my fucking leg …'

I remember my last ever fire call. I was lying in bed and there was this unmerciful explosion. A boy had driven a Land Rover-type vehicle to the door of the Killyhevlin Hotel where it went off and set the hotel on fire. The whole roof was on fire and the insulation in the walls, which was polystyrene, started burning. I had never seen this happen before. So, we couldn't put the blasted thing out. I knew Richard Watson, the owner, well, a lovely big man. We were parched and Richard was running about and he said, 'Boys, if you're hungry and down in the kitchen, pick up anything and eat it, and if you're going by the bar, don't be afraid to pour yourselves a drink.' So anyway, we were battling on – there were four or five of us with breathing apparatus and we were at the back near the bar, and I said to the boys, 'Have a drink – Richard told us. It's all above board.' So we all sat down at a table in the middle of all this mess with a drink and the next thing we see is this light approaching.

We all hid under the table and it was the divisional officer. He walked by but he never saw us. We had permission, like, but I wrote a letter to Richard to say thank you for making the refreshments available in case the divisional officer had seen us.

You could say I started my firefighting career with a bang and finished with a bang.

Ken Ramsey
Joined the retained service in Enniskillen in 1976.
I left Northern Ireland in the late sixties. I had worked at a newspaper in mid Ulster at the start of the Troubles – there wasn't shooting and killing, but there was civil strife, and friends on both sides were dividing. I couldn't see the point of it and I went to England. I was eighteen and discovered that England was a wonderful place, very free and easy – liberal, no politics, no religion. Then I came home and met my wife from Enniskillen. I am from a Protestant background and she is from a Catholic background, and even in those days people commented on it so we went to England.

Then the Troubles really started and I felt kind of out of it. My father was a firefighter in Enniskillen fire station. I was watching the news a lot and I thought it was wrong for me not to help in some way. My wife was of the same opinion and she also missed her family, so we came back to Enniskillen, and I told my father, who was retiring from the fire service, that I was going to join. He insisted I shave my beard off and cut my hair and that's what I did. I went through a very short recruitment process and I was a firefighter in the retained station in Enniskillen. I was given a pager and whenever there was an incident, controls in Lisburn got the information, and would automatically set off the pagers and the siren in Enniskillen. We would turn up and then the firefighters that were required on the fire appliance would go and attend the incident, wherever it was. At that time it was road accidents, house fires, farm and industrial accidents, and terrorist incidents as well. We were right out in the west of Northern Ireland, and there were no full-time firefighters – the only full-time firefighters were officers that came from division HQ. Being retained meant that even during the working day or at night at home, if the pager went off, you went to the incident. You would sort it out, come back to the fire station and you'd go straight back to work again or home. The incident could have been a road accident in which someone you knew was killed or involving someone's family that you knew. You just had to keep it to yourself and then go back and serve customers in your business – and that's how it was through my entire service in the retained.

We were one of the busiest retained fire stations in the British Isles and because the incidents grew, our skills grew, our ability to cope grew and the response times got shorter. So we really were a very busy station and we were also backing up more rural stations like Belleek and Irvinestown, and even every other fire station in Northern Ireland. Once a week we had a training session and then every so often we were sent off to the training centre in Belfast to improve our skills. If you got a rank you were sent off to the Fire Service National Training College in England at Morton-on-the-Marsh in Gloucestershire and it was a very special place. You really learned there. They were also impressed with us – one of the things they kept saying about Northern Ireland firefighters was that you couldn't keep them out of fires.

Very early one morning I was just getting up and an explosion went off. Because I hadn't been called to the fire station, I knew that it was a no-warning bomb. So I ran out of the house, got in my car and made my way to the fire station. At the station was a young firefighter, a very young fella, who'd come in obviously very shocked. The bomb had gone off under the car of this young fella's neighbour, who was a UDR soldier.

When you are driving towards an incident, all sorts of things are in your head. You're afraid of what you might see and who it might be. Is it someone you know? Is it a relative? Is there going to be another explosive device there? So all that is processing through your mind and then you look at the crew round you: you look at who are the toughest, who are the most skilled for particular jobs, who are the ones that are going to do this, who are the ones that are going to do that. The sub officer, who'd sit beside the driver, was looking round, sizing everyone up. He was calm and he was giving instructions and by the time we arrived, we were ready to go.

The UDR man was very badly trapped and his car had tangled up all round him. It wasn't far from the hospital and there was a doctor at the scene, a very young doctor, and he kept saying to me – because I was the one with the UDR man in the car – 'Don't let him pass out, don't let him go into shock, keep talking to him.' So I just talked and talked. God help that poor man – I don't know what I said to him but I kept talking and talking and I kept telling him, 'Don't drift off, come on, stay conscious.' I remember I gripped the steering wheel to do something and his hand came up and gripped my gloved hand and he couldn't, or wouldn't, let me go. I was stuck with him and that was it and the rest of the guys cut all the bits of the car away. To do it in a hurry, we tied one part of the car to the fire engine and one part to the ambulance and just drove them apart. Not standard practice, but that's what the sub officer made up his mind to do at the time and it worked very well. The only way I could get my hand back was to take my hand out and leave the glove – the soldier took my glove with him to the hospital.

I didn't know what happened for a long time, what his injuries were, although I did know he was alive. Purely coincidentally I met the doctor again and he told me that when they got to the Erne Hospital there was a consultant from Belfast there to give a lecture – a very famous doctor who was very well skilled in treating Troubles-related injuries, bomb explosion injuries and the like. This consultant wrote a list of instructions on a piece of paper and gave it to the doctor as they were putting the soldier and him into the helicopter to go to hospital in Belfast. Sometime during the journey this soldier started to lose consciousness so the doctor took out this bit of paper and followed the instructions in the middle of this helicopter journey, and gave him whatever injections, whatever treatment it said. The UDR soldier arrived in Belfast alive – that consultant's piece of paper saved his life.

Retained firefighters respond to incidents wherever they are required, but first and foremost, they serve locally. Inevitably this means that they often know or have a connection to the people they are trying to save – and sometimes that connection is heartbreakingly close.

When you got to the station for a fire call there was usually a printout with the address of the incident on it. You would look at the street and you would think, my brother lives there or my uncle lives there or my wife's family lives there or someone I know. A lot of the times you did know the people. You would go to an RTA and someone in the crew would say, that's such-and-such a person, somebody we all knew. That was part of the job we were in. It didn't make it any more difficult, but it would spur you on maybe.

The first time that it really struck home was the day one of my colleagues was taking a man out of a car and he realised it was his brother. That young man died. Part way through my career, on a nice sunny Sunday afternoon, my nephew – who loved fast cars – decided he would catch up with his friend who had gone on down the road in front of him. I don't know what happened but he hit a tree, the biggest tree on that road. He was dying and he was pretty messed up. I was taking him out of the car and I was aware that colleagues were pulling me back and I couldn't figure out why. 'I'm doing my job – what are you doing?' They were pulling me back and one of them said to me, 'That's your Darren, Ken.' I didn't know it was my own nephew. And when I looked up I saw this parked car down the road and it was my brother-in-law and his wife, the young lad's mother and father. Somebody had phoned them up and said, 'Darren's after crashing his car.' At that time, thank goodness, he was alive, so I didn't have to tell them anything I didn't want to but I learned from that never to tell people lies in any situation. If someone asked you 'Is my wife okay?' you would avoid saying some things – you would just say, 'We are concentrating on the job right now, there's somebody else dealing with your wife,' because our job was to save lives. We were not trained to break the news that someone has died.

On 8 November 1987, a Provisional IRA bomb exploded near the cenotaph in Enniskillen during the town's Remembrance Day service. Twelve people died and sixty-three were injured.
Normally I would be down at the war memorial early, but that year I had torn the ligaments in my leg playing football, so I was late. The bomb went off and I was a good distance away, but not that far so I started to run towards it. I met a policeman and asked him what had happened. He said, 'A bomb's gone off, Ken, and no warning.'

I said, 'Are people hurt?'

He said, 'A lot, a lot,' so I turned round and ran to the fire station. We have a direct line to our control room and I picked it up and I told the control operator that a no-warning bomb had gone off. This was minutes, moments, after it had exploded. I told the control room that there were a lot of casualties and a building had collapsed. The operator told me to stay there. She set off the alarms and the first crew came in and I stayed on the phone – it was more important for me to stay on the phone. She asked me for as much information as I could give her because they were assessing the situation, even at this early stage, to see if it was a major incident. Then I went off and started helping at the scene up the street.

I remember black clouds of dust and the usual panic among people. We came up behind the first crew that had arrived – an officer in charge of that crew was making plans. The building had collapsed on top of lots of people so you had a lot of crush injuries. There was a metal railing that had trapped people. I was given orders and told what to do, and then I was given a crew and I gave them orders as to what to do and the best way to do it. We had to form a wedge because there were hundreds of people trying to help those who were trapped, but they were climbing over things, they were pulling at things. There was no order, there was no discipline, so we had to very carefully get a line in between them and make use of people in the best way. 'You do this', 'You do that', 'Be careful of this', 'Just get in there,' – we were supervising and directing all of the rescuers and then ourselves as well.

We were doing what we had been trained to do. I didn't have any thoughts as to whether this was a shocking incident or the scale of it – we were just doing our job and concentrating on getting people out and helping them to stay alive. As time went by I remember stepping back to look round. You're continually assessing, and you're looking at the rest of the building thinking, is it going to fall on the rescuers? So two or three of us were tasked with keeping an eye on the building. We were doing a bit then watching the building and everything else. People were running towards us – 'Did you see this?' 'Did you see that?'

In the middle of all this I remember watching a primary school child who was just standing still. Someone who stands still in a panic situation sticks out. Everyone else was running around but this child was just standing there and I remember thinking to myself, what's that child doing there? I went down to him and I said, 'Are you okay?' I was trying to figure out if he was injured when he said, 'I lost my uncle.' I think he had been brought to lay a wreath for the school at the war memorial because he was quite close to it at the time the bomb went off. So I said, 'You stand here with me,' and I reached down and he held my hand. I'm standing in the middle of all this just holding this child's hand, talking to him. I said, 'You'll be okay – someone will be along to collect you in a little while,' and then through the crowd I saw this man running in absolute panic. He came running up and he was shouting and I realised he was shouting at the boy. Even in that situation part of my mind was saying, I've got to make sure this man is with the child. You can't just hand over a child. So I said, 'Are you a relative of this child?' and he said, 'Yes, I'm his uncle.' He was kind of angry with me. But I knew this man to see – not exactly who he was but to see – so I gave the child to him and he grabbed him up in his arms and fled out through the rubble and the mayhem.

We worked on. I remember there was a casualty on the ground and someone was down beside them, about to put a coat over their head. I said, 'I'm not sure – how do you know that person's dead?' I pulled the coat back and looked at the person and thought there was something; that they weren't dead. I started to shout, 'Is there a doctor? I need a doctor' – you just shout out, you know. There's no central station where you go and dial 'I need a doctor'. These two guys came through the crowd and they were army doctors – well, one of them was and the other was his medical orderly. I realised by the way they were working with the casualty that he was very desperately hurt, but they kept him alive for five more minutes, ten more minutes. I remember watching them – I was making sure nobody bothered them and that nothing would fall on them either – and I remember thinking to myself, if I get hurt these are the guys I want. They were absolutely phenomenally good.

A colleague came along and I was talking to him when

I saw one of our crew, a firefighter, standing still in the middle of the street. I went over and I said, 'Seamus, are you okay?' Then he pointed down and he was standing with his feet on either side of a body part, the most essential part a person can have. It was just sitting on the ground between his feet. I said, 'Okay, don't move, stay there. I'll come back.' So I went looking and I found a young police officer and I said, 'Have you got bags for body parts?' He ran to a police car and he came back with a plastic body-parts bag. There's a special way to hold this sort of bag: you fold the opening around your hands so that you and the body part don't make contact and don't get contaminated. We made him hold the bag like that and we lifted the body part up and set it inside, and as we did that he fainted, he just started to go. We knew just looking at him, so we moved to each side of him and we linked under his arms and we held him up and he came to after a few seconds. He was apologising, saying, 'Guys, I'm sorry. I didn't expect that; I didn't know.' We just said, 'It's okay, don't worry.' We made sure he was okay and then he went away with the bag.

Shortly after, I met my cousin who was in the security forces and he was looking for his wife. His wife was in, I think, the Red Cross or the St John's Ambulance. She was at the cenotaph when the bomb exploded and he couldn't find her. He asked me if I had seen her and I said I hadn't. He was really distressed and panicking. He said, 'I've been to the hospital, Ken, I can't find her in the hospital.' If you can't find someone in the hospital, either they're somewhere at the scene or they're in the morgue. I told him that there was a temporary morgue in the Territorial Army base so he went there. Later, he came back and found me again and said, 'I found her, she's alive, I found her, Ken.'

There were two ladies in Enniskillen whose house was right opposite the War Memorial. Everyone in the town called them the Miss Kavanaghs. They had opened their doors to help and I walked a casualty over to their house. It was someone covered with blood but who was walking and fit to move around. There were injured people on chairs in the ladies' kitchen and medics and the Miss Kavanaghs were treating people there. I remember looking at the floor and it was completely red with blood. Those two ladies were absolutely brilliant and I never found out how they got cleaned up or what happened after or who talked to them or thanked them or what.

We were sad, really sad. This was an incident that happened when we thought we were heading for peace, things were rolling that way. We weren't shocked, because it had happened to us before, but we were shocked that someone would still have that thought in their head. A senior officer had a road accident on the way to the bomb. I remember getting in touch with him on the radio as it was important for him to be there for all sorts of reasons. When you're an officer you want to be there. Now the intensity of the situation, the heat, was over, but brigade officers – high-ranking officers – still hadn't arrived. This officer was one of ours, we knew him and we liked him. He was about twelve or fourteen miles out of town, so we took the smallest fire engine and two of us went and fetched him. We were talking to him on the way back to Enniskillen about what had happened, filling him in so that when he arrived at the scene he didn't have to be briefed again; he arrived there ready to go. When he got there he took over and became the senior officer at the scene. Other brigade officers arrived but they had a different role.

Then it became obvious that we were completely exhausted and that we weren't needed any more. It was a very big crime scene and there were crews brought down to relieve us. We went back to the fire station and had a chat and I think I might even have had a cigarette. I remember afterwards that we had news and media people wanting to come into the station to interview us, but none of us would speak to them. There was no plan that we wouldn't talk to them but we just said no. We were conscious that this was a community sticking together irrespective of religion or faith or even politics, this was our community gathering round. I remember the day after, or at one of the funerals, no one in Enniskillen would talk to the newspaper people or the TV companies who came from all over the world. That's typical of Enniskillen – everyone knows each other.

I was, and still am, full of admiration for the Enniskillen people and deeply respect the families who lost their fathers and mothers and sons and uncles and aunts. Some of them were very young but I buried all that a long time ago in my head; I had to.

In the days after it happened I went home from work to get changed into my fire service uniform, went to a funeral, came back to work, went to another funeral, and that went on for nearly a week.

Dungannon

Like many towns, Dungannon suffered significantly during the Troubles. There were numerous bomb and incendiary attacks on commercial buildings and serious, often fatal, attacks on the security forces in the wider area. Sectarian violence was also, sadly, all too common. The local retained fire station was stretched on many occasions and the crews knew that assistance from the nearest stations would take time to arrive.

Gordon Cuddy
Joined the retained fire service in the town in 1978.
My very first call was an unofficial one. We had three pumping appliances in the station at that time. Two pumps

were called out to a hayshed, which left only one in the station to cover the town. Then a call came in at approximately one o'clock in the morning. The bad guys, as I would call them nowadays, had broken into the local bus depot and set numerous buses alight and there were only three or four men on station. So being the keen young lad, I heard the siren that night and thought I'd go up and see what's going on. A certain leading firefighter, I will not mention his name, said, 'Right young Cuddy, time to earn your corn! Grab your kit – you're coming out on a call.' By the time we pulled up at the scene the buses were going well. On this particular night everything was kicking off and we only had five firemen and one pump. There was very little backup to be had from anywhere in Northern Ireland, so we had to tackle it on our own – we pumped water on to it for most of the night.

So, I did my training right through and got my breathing apparatus course. I think it was 1981 when the bad guys broke in and set several incendiaries in a big warehouse in the Granville Industrial Estate. If there was no traffic on the road, you could be out turning the wheel on the first pump in about five or six minutes. In those days you had to drive around the town to get into the station because there were only two access points – all the other routes to the centre were blocked off by security gates. From where I lived, I had to go around the town and up Quarry Lane into Thomas Street. The rest of them had to do the same coming from various other directions. For a bomb in the square, everyone from the Moygashel side of the town had to go right round the chapel. It was bedlam sometimes when traffic wouldn't let you through. Anyway, we got three or four pump appliances to the fire. Back then you just grabbed your breathing apparatus and piled in. If you were told to jump high, you jumped. Myself and a colleague went in to the building with a fully charged seventy millimetre hose – we got to the fire, knocked it down and then we opened up to ventilate the place. Later the police searched the place properly and found two more incendiaries in the building. These were not small incendiaries – they were jam jars full of fuel with a bomb and detonator attached, capable of causing a heck of a lot of damage. An officer brought one of them out and looked at me and said, 'You were in there with that thing.' It was a bit of a wake-up call – you were basically just a young fella enjoying your work but you didn't know what you were getting yourself into.

I went on a few more calls and the Troubles were really getting going. Coalisland was a certain hot spot for trouble so we were down there regularly for car fires and other incidents. One night two pumps were called down. I was driving the second pump as a convoy and there was a fairly good distance between me and the pump in front. The next thing I knew the driver in the first pump slammed on the brakes and I was up his tailpipe, nearly into the back of him. Then he slammed the reversing lights on. It transpired that some suspicious people had stepped into the middle of the road with what looked like a weapon and had pointed it at the pump, so the sub officer said. 'Let's get out of here.' Whatever was on fire, those guys didn't want it put out, so we withdrew to a safe location and asked the police to get it sorted before we could go back and deal with it. I can never forget those reversing lights coming on and him coming back at me very quickly.

On the plus side of things, the camaraderie and the craic in the wagon were exceptional. You had young hands like myself, keen as mustard, and the experienced hands trying to do the job. You were going to jobs at one or two o'clock in the morning and coming back at six or seven for a quick shower and breakfast before heading back out to other jobs. You were buggered. When you went out at night back in those days, you knew you were going to a job. You knew you would be out for hours. Back then there were no relief crews about. You were at the job until it was done – you were doing up to ten-hour stints. All you had were your basic debris gloves, woolly jacket, cork hat, plastic leggings and a pair of boots. On a cold winter's night, you were bloody cold. But over a period of time the power that be started to invest in the kit, and I must give them credit – now the kit is second to none compared to when I joined. I compliment them on that and the kit on the wagons. The wagons themselves are fantastic. In those days you had the breathing apparatus set in a yellow box on the back of the wagon and when you pulled up to a 'persons reported' you had to jump out, pull out a box, put on a set, do your check and go in, whereas now you can do it all on the way to the call.

Even in the middle of the Troubles, the ordinary stuff kept happening. We have a stretch of road here called the Old Ballygawley Road, and we were out maybe three times a month with RTCs. It was a notorious stretch of road. People were killed and people were injured and some of the scenes and some of the stuff we had to deal with … At one particular incident I was a temporary sub officer. We got an RTC call for a car wrapped round a fairly large tree. We pulled up and we got the driver and the passenger out, but the young cub in the back seat nearest the tree, he was badly pinned. He wasn't coming out. So the guys got to work with every piece of kit they had: rams, cutters, hacksaws, screwdrivers and everything. While that was happening, I was standing back with another firefighter, and the mother turns up. That was a challenging situation. She wasn't allowed to go near the car and she was going ape. To cut a long story short, we got the cub out and to the ambulance. He was critically injured. Wind the clock forward maybe two years and I was standing in the local confectionery shop waiting to buy my paper. A young fella walks up to me and shakes my hand, so I asked, 'Do I know you?' and he said, 'You should do, you cut me out of that car two years ago.' He thanked me profusely and thanked the crews involved. That was a heart-warming type of thing, where you got a wee bit of appreciation from the community – and for all the guys, not only myself. We are here for the community, we work round the town, we talk to them, we know them and they know us as well.

The brigade was often called out to incidents at which it was far from clear what was going on or what had happened, and often it was a case of doing whatever needed to be done without asking too many questions. One such incident took place at Clonoe Chapel near Coalisland on 16 February 1992.

We often had to drive around the country at night and so we often came across soldiers and police doing checkpoints. About 90 per cent of the time they just waved you through but there were times when things were not so straightforward. There was one situation at Clonoe chapel. The IRA had attacked the local police station in Coalisland and then had driven back to the car park beside the chapel in Clonoe. The police and security forces were waiting for them, and four IRA men lost their lives that day. Some of the tracer rounds set the chapel alight, so we had to go in and make sure the fire was out and then leave quickly – don't get involved, don't talk to any of the people around you and don't make any comments. That was an odd situation to be in: you couldn't talk to anybody, especially not to the locals who were congregating. The police were there and a lot of other people – who they were, I don't know and don't want to know. We just did the job and left.

Firefighters turn out to help others but sometimes need help themselves, and it could, on occasions, be a close call as to which they were – responders or victims.

The business that my father set up back in 1950 was bombed twice. As a result, the family used to take turns to do firebomb watch. You went in at about twelve o'clock at night and got home at about half three – the bombs were normally timed to go off between twelve and three to maximise damage. I remember I was there on my watch, sitting in the shop and reading a book. At about half-two in the morning somebody came rattling the door. It was the security guy from Wellworths next door and he says, 'There's a fire! There's a fire in Wellworths!' So I ripped in and there was a pretty well-developed fire taking hold. I rang the fire service and ran over to the station across the square. I had the three engine-room doors open and my kit already on waiting to roll out and when the other boys arrived. They said, 'Where did you come from?' I said, 'There is a fire over in Wellworths – let's get over there and get this damn thing put out.' They were asking how I was there so bloody quick, even J.B. Johnston, and he only lived down the street! I'd been sitting in my own business minding my own business, but that guy ran in to find me because he knew I was a fireman.

Throughout the Troubles, we got it from both sides of the community because we went into situations regardless of who it was that needed help. We were there to help people; we were not there to create any discontent; we were not making a political scene. If there was a fire to put out, we put it out, or if there was a life to be saved, we saved that life – it didn't matter if it was a Hindu, Catholic, Protestant or whatever else, we just went and sorted it out. But it could be scary. Another time there was trouble and a fire in Coalisland. It was 4 a.m. – the riot was already put to bed and the police had the place cleared. I was standing in a field of debris on my own and went to put a hydrant in down the road. I had the hydrant in and I was looking round myself and thinking that someone was watching me. I was spooked that night. There were bottles lying about the place, there were burning cars and I was setting up a hydrant and nobody round me, not a sinner. I thought to myself, I'm getting this thing set up and the hose rolled out and I'm getting the hell out of here. It was one of those times when I felt like someone was watching me and I felt a bit on my own.

Firefighters are at the scenes of, and work at, terrible incidents that are hugely traumatic, but a deep camaraderie and the sustained support of their families are of a value beyond measure.

On the Troubles side of things, I coped reasonably well with all those early mornings and late nights when I was young and keen as mustard, but as time went on and I got a bit wiser, I let the youngsters go out instead. When the peace came, the variety of stuff we were dealing with changed; the demands on the service diminished somewhat. Back in the dark days of the Troubles you needed a lot of machines to run about the country – I went all over the place to do fire calls – but once the peace came and the Good Friday Agreement came, the calls we were doing were more ordinary: automatic fire alarms, an odd chimney fire, traffic accidents, and so on.

When it was bad, I saw a lot of people killed and that did take its toll on me. At one stage I wasn't coping. I was for leaving – that was me, I'd had enough – but there was a certain station officer who took me aside and talked to me. We had a few phone calls, and I went for a pint the odd time with him. He got me back on the straight and narrow. I'm glad he did because I would've missed it. It was tough times then. I owe him a debt of gratitude.

Everyone has their own perspective and their own personal experience of the fire service. For me, when I came here, I just enjoyed the work. I enjoyed the camaraderie in the back of the wagon at two o'clock in the morning – some ugly faces and some less so! I was in the front seat for about twenty-five years as leading firefighter. I'd look round at the guys behind me and I'd know that all of them were up to speed, so if I said two BAs and a jet, I didn't need to say who was going to do it – the boys just got stuck in. Our current watch commander runs the station very well. Overall I have enjoyed my forty-plus years in the service. I will be going out in a couple of weeks' time, so I will miss it! I certainly will miss it, but I am not young enough or supple enough to do the job any more. In my opinion, anybody who does this job wants to serve the community, and they join a group of guys who don't mind getting stuck in and doing the job. They want to help, they want to do something for their community.

I can't express my gratitude enough to all of our wives, girlfriends and partners – whatever you want to call them – over the years. When that bleeper goes off, most of the guys are away. From my own experience, my wife put up with many nights sitting at home watching TV by herself, maybe worrying, while the kids were in bed. Even with only two kids I've missed several important family events because of going out on calls. I can't praise my family enough – if they can put up with all that, they can put up with almost anything. Now with me retiring in a few weeks' time my wife is going to be sick of me. She'll wish I'd stayed for another while!

Firefighter Hugh Kennedy being assisted at the scene of the collapse of the Melville Hotel in 1971 in which two colleagues died.

THE NORTH-WEST

Derry/Londonderry

Regardless of their religion or political affiliation, the people of Derry/Londonderry have a deep sense of connection to their city. This is true also of the firefighters who served there.

When things deteriorated in 1969 and civil unrest became more widespread and severe, the local fire station was very much on the 'front line'. Up to this point, fire engines (and their crews) had never been attacked, but this changed quite suddenly and crews had to adapt to a new reality. The city suffered a great deal over the subsequent years and many bombs and fires left their mark. Dealing with the divisions in the city required a sensitivity – and level of diplomacy – from the crews and their officers. It's a tribute to their professionalism that, despite these acute local difficulties, the service was maintained through even the very worst days.

Hugh Kennedy

Joined the full-time service in 1965. For most of his service, he was based in Northland Road Fire Station in Derry/Londonderry. He remembers one of the first attacks on the fire brigade in the city.

When I started in 1965 it was haysheds and chimney fires. That was it. There was the odd house fire and the odd derelict house fire because a lot of the properties were falling into disrepair around the city at the time. It bounced from that to the start of the Troubles because all the civil rights business was starting to happen. But I lived on the East Bank, which is on the Waterside, and we knew very little about what was going on on the West Bank. One Saturday when I was due to start duty at six o'clock, I left my house to drive to the fire station and I saw all these water marks on the bridge. When I got to the station I was asked, 'Oh, did you not know there was a civil rights march today?' I says, 'No. What was all the water for?' 'That was the water cannons,' I was told. I didn't know what a water cannon was! But anyway, there we were, at the start of the Troubles.

That night I was in the control room when we got a fire call to part of the Lecky Road and we turned out two fire engines. Normally, in those days, you had to go to the nearest telephone to phone back to say what was happening on the fire ground. Nowadays it's sophisticated with radios and all that there. In those days you had to find a telephone. The two teams were gone for a couple of hours. I was sitting in the control room on my own, wondering where the heck everybody had gone.

Turned out they were attacked on Lecky Road. And two of the fire engines had taken boys to hospital – some of their crew. A guy walked back to the fire station on his own from the Bog, from Lecky Road area. 'We were attacked!' he told me.

I said 'Who? Who would attack you?' You know, this was unheard of.

He says, 'Ah, the Bog crowd attacked us.'

I said, 'What? Why?'

He says, 'Well, you know about those water cannons that were on the bridge today? They associated us with the water cannons.'

They thought we had supplied them, but it wasn't us – it was the police.

Some of the guys were quite badly injured – they'd been hit by stones. But you know, we quickly learnt not to just drive into an area. Don't forget, that was only in the very early stages of the Troubles. So it was a learning curve from then on in. And when we had to have some rapport with the people we went down and said to them, 'When you need the fire brigade, we'll be there. We're not part of the structure of government, police and army. We're not part of it. We're a civilian force.' And to take the thing even further we weren't allowed metal screens on the fire engines. The only concession that we were allowed was to harden the windscreen. We replaced normal glass with a type of perspex that couldn't be broken with stones. We didn't want to become militarised. That's the word I would use. Once you put metal grilles up and all that there, you become militarised. We weren't – we were a civilian fire brigade.

That first attack – that was the most ferocious attack that I ever saw on the fire brigade. We still got the odd one when we went up the wrong street or down the wrong road. And you would have the odd youth wanting to have a go at you with a stone here or there. But the general public got to learn that they needed the fire brigade. The message that we were not going to be militarised came from the Fire Brigades Union and once we got that message over, things changed. I could name a number of incidents that happened right in those areas where we were needed very badly in similar circumstances, to deal with the Troubles. Some of the loss of life that happened in areas like the Creggan, there was nobody else there to deal with these incidents other than the fire brigade. I'm jumping years here, but it became a no-go area. And we would have driven up to a barricade. The people manning the barricade would have had the nod that there was a fire a couple of blocks away in big estates like the Creggan. So they knew: pull the barrier. But they sometimes decided to escort us. Somebody would get into the fire engine and make sure you weren't part of the military, and sometimes they would have asked you to speak a few words to check you didn't have an English accent. It was all, 'We know you, we know who you are.' Derry is a small place. So they quickly got to know who the fire crews were. Because we were in the civilian fire brigade, what we had to go and do we had to go and do: didn't matter who was involved or whose life was at risk. We were still going to go.

You have to understand that there was a lot of other stuff going on: chimney fires were still happening, derelict house fires were happening. But then sometimes there was an incident where the rioting got a bit more serious – they would have decided to burn down a factory or burn down some other structure – and it became tense. My recollection of Troubles-related incidents wouldn't be something I would wish to speak about in case that would be offensive to some people.

They were constructing a new police station on the Strand Road a long while after the Troubles began. Our fire station was just above where they were building. One afternoon we got a call: there was an old gas yard over in the Bogside, but they were closing the gas yard down, so they were bringing the gas from Belfast in tankers. We got a call to say there was a gas tanker outside the police station that was under construction, and there were bombs on it. So, we got in the fire engines, dropped down the two hundred metres from the fire station, down Lawrence Hill, turned round the corner and we could see this big gas truck sitting. Now on every truck like this there is a Hazchem code to tell you what the lorry is carrying and the code on that one said GAS – that was fair enough, right? The boss man phoned the gas company and asked them about the tanker and the procedure we should follow. The person at the gas company said, 'How far are you from the gas tanker?'

'We're sitting looking at it.'

He says, 'You should evacuate the area for one square mile.'

If you ever saw a fire engine going to a fire call at full speed, you can imagine how that looks in reverse … we made the quickest exit ever. Turned the fire engines right round, and stopped about half a mile down the road. The gas tanker exploded causing a firestorm. It didn't do the police station much damage because it was still under construction.

The army had two sentries up on each side of the police station to protect the building workers and there were two factories on this side of the street. By the time the gas tanker exploded, the soldiers had already vacated the two army posts but they had left all the ammunition behind them. And the firestorm drove the fire through these two factory units. If you've seen a Californian forest fire, that's what a firestorm looks like. And we came back up with the fire trucks, and all the ammunition was going off at the sentry posts. So we were in a kind of limbo-land, stuck between trying to put the fire out and trying to not get shot.

Ashes is what was left of the buildings. They were finished. That's what a firestorm does, it drives the fire through the building, through glass, through walls, through gateways. On the other side of the factories was the quayside, the River Foyle. We were able to go to the river and start pumping water to put the factory out. We knew how to deal with a gas fire. You let it burn. You don't try and put a gas fire out because you could drive the thing down and even cause another explosion. So we kept the area round it cold, spraying water on it. And then we were firefighting the factories. It was total devastation. It was like the Blitz, not that I remember it, but I have seen photos. A major incident. I think we were there for about three days.

There was a catalogue of events, you know? That was one event. The the next day there would be another event. Then the next night there would be another event. And then you might have had a car crash. That was a whole different scenario. You had to be aware of Troubles-related incidents, and then you had to be aware of the ordinary firefighting duties that we have every day in a fire station: peoples' houses going on fire, chip pans going on fire, and so on.

Even in the midst of the Troubles, the 'routine' work didn't stop. While crews could be dealing with an incident that was difficult because of the uniqueness of Northern Ireland's civil unrest, controls could urgently need them for the 'bread-and-butter' incidents – many of which were as urgent as any Troubles-related call.
In the nationalist area of the city, 15 August is bonfire night. There were bonfires in the Creggan area, and we got a call to one at one o'clock in the morning. We went to the scene,

but you don't actually put a bonfire out. You just dampen the area around it and stand back in case something major goes wrong. We had two fire trucks at it. I was in charge of one truck, and my colleague was in charge of the other. He was there first. He said to me, 'Head you back to the station, we'll just deal with this.' On my way back to the fire station I got a radio message from control to say to turn out to basically the same area: a house fire. I thought that maybe they were talking about that bonfire again because people get confused when they see smoke They had given me the name of a street beside where the bonfire was and when we arrived, there was smoke coming out of the front door. A lady and a gentleman were standing at the door very much in distress. He says, 'My kids, my kids, my kids, they're upstairs!'

Unless you're in these incidents you don't understand how panicky the whole thing is and, as the fire brigade, you've got to keep calm. Other people all around you are excited, but if you keep calm, you're going to deal with it. I had two breathing apparatus men ready and they went to the bedroom up the stairs and brought the two kids down. They had woken them out of their sleep. This all occurred within two or three minutes: landing, getting the kids out, getting them in the ambulance and away to the hospital. The mother and the father went with them.

When we got the situation all cleared, it turned out that it wasn't a big fire. The washing machine had been put underneath the worktop too tight, and the motor had set the worktop on fire. The only smoke was the smoke from the worktop but that can be quite deadly. When we had everything cleared up we went up to check the rooms. Where our boys had lifted the kids, the bits where their heads had been on the pillows were white. The rest of the pillow was black. That's how lucky those kids were.

The parents came back and we had a bit of a chat outside, as you do. 'The kids are fine,' the dad says. 'They're just keeping them in for observation.' I'm not going to repeat the language he used, but he was very excited that we had saved his kids. And we were proud of being able to assist in that kind of situation. But he said to me, 'Come here till I show you, let me show you this here.' He opened the garage door and showed me his vehicle: cases and all in the back. He says, 'We were leaving for holiday in the morning.'

'Well, do you know what to do?' I says to him. 'You leave for your holiday in the morning. Because you see that damage done there, it's no big damage: bit of smoke and that there. You get the kids out of hospital in the morning, get them dressed, and away you go on your holidays!'

And he turned round and he says 'I think I will.'

That was a normal thing – the bonfire was a political thing but this was a normal fire call. The two incidents happened within minutes of each other. That's the fire brigade; that's the way it goes.

The Troubles massively increased the number and severity of incidents the fire brigade were attending and, as a result, in Derry/ Londonderry firefighters agreed to come in off duty when things got particularly tight. Hugh Kennedy was one of those who responded on 21 November 1971 to a fire in the Melville Hotel at which two firefighters, Lexie Wylie and Leonard McCartney, lost their lives.
I'll share this story reluctantly because, of all my days in the fire brigade, it was one of the worst. A lot of other incidents happened, but that one still gives me a great deal of pain.

I was off duty that night. My brother was in the fire brigade at the time as well. We were both off duty. In those days, because of the Troubles, we had been given alerters – bleepers to let us know if the fire station needed extra help; for reserve people to come in. So anyway, we were out that night, as you do on a Saturday night – a good old night out. We came back to my mum's house and had a cup of tea. There was no drinking and all in those days. Those things didn't happen then.

Sometime in the middle of the night, the bleepers went. By this time we had got used to the bleepers going. So we took the car over, and drove down along the quay, along the Foyle River, and there was quite a bit of smoke. Initially, we thought it was fog coming from the water, but it was smoke coming from the Melville Hotel. But we didn't go to the fire straightaway, we had to go to the fire station first, because that's how the control worked. It wasn't like, aw, we'll drop off here, we'll drop off there. At the station was a Green Goddess – one of the old ex-army fire engines we used to keep. All the rest of the fire engines were gone and they were wanting more help. That's why we were called on the bleepers. My brother got into the first Green Goddess, along with three or four other boys. They made up a crew and off they went. Because I was there, and a couple of other boys were there, somebody said to me, 'Go and help the guy in the control room.' (We had a small control room there in the city.) So I went in there and helped. This was a fairly normal big fire at the Melville hotel. Everybody was relaxed about it, you know? A big fire's a big fire. That's how you deal with it: more fire engines. So, as the night progressed, things sort of quietened down at our end because all the action was happening at the Melville Hotel.

First of all we got a message back, through the telephones, to say that the fire was under control. Great. No problem. That's what we used to call a stop message – everything's over and nearly sorted out. But within maybe ten or fifteen minutes – I can't remember the exact time – we got a message back to the control room to say, 'Building collapsed; persons reported trapped.' Well, my heart jumped because there was nobody else there going to be trapped, only firemen. I had to get out of that control room. We pressed the bleeper again and got one or two other boys to come. We had another fire engine sitting there, so we got into that and went down to the Melville Hotel. And, of course, the first thing I asked was, 'Where's my brother? Where's Jackie?' Everybody knew each other.

'Oh, he's up at the turntable ladder,' someone replied.

There was a fierce fire burning at the top at that stage and the wind had got up.

So then, I was taking instructions from the bosses on where to go to search for people, and I was told to go to this one particular area along with some of the other boys. I had a good idea of the layout of the Melville Hotel because I had been in it before but this time there was no going through the front door. We were going in the windows on the ground floor. We started to search, and you can imagine the confusion and the noise, and nobody knew at this stage who was lost.

We went in, and then somebody said to me, 'It's Leonard McCartney.' Leonard McCartney and me were very big pals. He had been talking to me the night before in the fire station. He had taken over a small family business, and had been trying to gather up money to run the business. Somebody added, 'And we think it's likely Lexie Wylie as well.' Those were the two boys that were trapped. Under those circumstances, you shout out people's names, hoping that someone will answer you, so I started to shout, 'Leonard! Leonard! Leonard!' and this voice shouted back to me, 'I'm all right!' but it was another Leonard from Strabane Fire Station that I also knew very well. So my heart went up and down. This Leonard appeared out of the dust and smoke and, as he did, another part of the ceiling fell down. Me and the boys around me got badly hit with this other material coming down. Somewhere there's footage of me being taken out of the Melville Hotel by another colleague of mine from Strabane, and a soldier, as the army were there helping us as well.

I started to gather my thoughts, and as I wasn't very badly injured, I thought to myself, right, I'm going to go back in again, but one of my senior bosses told me that nobody was to go back in. I fell out with him because my emotions were right up there. I says, 'You know, we're not going to leave – you can't do that.' And he said, 'I'll speak to you in a minute.' That was a guy who was much senior to me telling me, 'Well, you're wrong.' It was very hard for me to be told I was wrong when my friend was buried somewhere in there but the guy was exactly right. He didn't want me to become a casualty again, which was a risk because all this structure had burned away. Other colleagues of mine had been in different positions that night when the collapse had happened originally and were all on the street fairly badly hurt – they all had to be taken away to hospital. There was an awful lot of confusion and then there was an awful, deadly silence. I can still remember it now.

We went back to the fire station in the morning and we still didn't know how those boys were going to be recovered. We had the army with bulldozers, but because the high walls were still standing, you couldn't just go in and bulldoze and pull them all down. It had to be done in a very controlled way.

My brother, who had been at the fire initially, drove the fire engine that carried Leonard McCartney's coffin on top.

That was the Melville Hotel fire. It still hurts me but it hurt me even more at the time because I had young children, and so had Leonard McCartney. Passage of time has probably helped and an awful lot has happened to me in my lifetime since. But I mean, that kind of thing would never leave your mind. The way it was in the Troubles, whenever you finished – there was no debriefing, no 'go and see a psychologist'. The psychologist we went to was the local pub! And that was about it.

Billy Hamilton
Joined the full-time service in Derry/Londonderry in 1969, initially serving at Northland Road in the city.
There was a guy had a television shop on the Strand Road

and two guys came in from the Provisional IRA and left a bomb with him and went out again. He promptly lifted the bomb and took it out to the street. After liaising with our senior officers and the ATO, we were instructed to set up a ground monitor and disperse the bomb from a safe distance. Now a ground monitor is a large jet of water that can be left unattended and allows us to withdraw, so we just put the ground monitor on the bomb, dispersed it, and then went back to the station – and that was it.

A couple of days later we got a call to a chimney fire in the Bogside Inn. At that time nobody could get in to the Bogside area without the IRA's say-so – they had their own checkpoint set up. I think even the bin collections had been suspended by the council. When the crew were turned out to the Bogside Inn they were told by the Provisional IRA to clean the street – 'You were able to clean the Strand Road, so you can get your hoses out and clean this street'. There was no violence or intimidation or nothing. I think they were just letting us know that they knew we had dispersed the bomb. At the end of it all, the boys who went down even received a bottle of whiskey to take back to the station ...

Things did get difficult – especially in the Bogside. If they wanted you in, you had no trouble getting in at all. It was only if they had barricades up – buses or vans they had stolen – that you knew they didn't want you in. It would depend on what you were going to or what you were attending. Then when it was dealt with, you would have probably got stoned when you were leaving. It was like recreational rioting to some people.

Billy also vividly remembers the fire at the Melville Hotel.
Of all the incidents I attended, the only one I can remember the date of is the Melville Hotel: 21 November 1971. Everybody was there. Because of the situation in the city then, we regularly had to bring in Strabane and Limavady to back us up. It was a Saturday night, I was off duty and

the alerter went off. My wife was due to give birth – our daughter arrived two weeks after that incident – so initially I wasn't going to go, but I knew it was going to be something big, so I made my way up to Northland Station. There was a spare appliance and whoever turned in was getting sent down to the fire at the Melville Hotel straightaway. The thing that sticks in my mind is that I was probably the last person to speak to the two firemen that were killed, Lexie Wylie and Leonard McCartney. I was speaking to them a short time before the floors collapsed. A more senior fireman called Alex Kay came in and asked me to give him a hand with something. Bearing in mind I was only two years in the job and he was more senior, I did what I was told. I went with him and we were actually in the foyer of the hotel when the floors collapsed. The doorway right beside us completely filled with rubble and we ended up in the street. It caught us unawares. It was well above my pay scale to ask questions about what went wrong – I don't think we ever found out to be honest with you. I never heard the real cause of the fire. To make matters worse for me, I was on nights the next night, the Sunday night, and we were sent down to the hotel again. I was there when they got the bodies out. It was the military that actually located the bodies and brought them out and there was men all standing crying. I was one of them.

Aubrey Crawford

Spent all of his service in Derry/Londonderry and had a horrifying experience of the Troubles very early in his career, in December 1974.
I joined the brigade in April 1974. We trained for nine weeks then were appointed to our various watches. I was Red Watch and on the day in question we'd had lunch and were preparing to go out on afternoon duties, whatever those might have been at the time. There were a number of us standing in the duty office, including Divisional

Commander Charlie Bell. We heard this dull explosion and out the window we could see smoke curling from the window of a building close to the fire station. Without even going through the control room, Charlie Bell told us to proceed to the incident.

As we rushed up the stairs we could hear this young woman screaming. I was one of the first to get to the top of the stairs and the scene that met us was horrendous. We thought there had possibly been a gas explosion – but we soon learned what this young lady had been doing. A guy, the bomb maker, had made letter bombs and she was there to take them to the post office and post them. As she'd been packing these bombs into her bag, they'd exploded and the scene that met us will live with me forever. This young lady had awful injuries – the sort of appalling damage that only a bomb can inflict. It was horrendous just to look. The tips of her fingers had all been blown off and they were a bloody mess.

Before joining the brigade I had been in nursing and the crew knew that I had a bit of experience, so I was left, and I mean left, to render first aid, which was very difficult. In fact, I remember Charlie Bell coming up the stairs to ask what had happened. I had covered the young lady to try to stop her seeing the injuries that she had – and when I showed them to Charlie Bell he put up his hands and turned away. He too left and I had to deal with this young lady.

Waiting on the ambulance to come seemed to take forever. Eventually it arrived and the young lady was put on a stretcher and taken down the stairs. I was ordered by Charlie Bell to go in the ambulance with Dr McCabe – who was the brigade doctor at the time and had come on the scene – and a local priest who had been passing. We all three of us went in the ambulance. The priest was administering the Last Rites. Dr McCabe and myself were trying to do what we could and it was quite limited. But the thing that I do remember, and you'll forgive me if I get upset: to this day I can still hear that young lady crying out in pain. It wasn't a hardened terrorist that I was seeing; she was a young woman with horrendous injuries and the only thing that she cried for was her mammy. She never lost consciousness as we travelled in the ambulance and I was at her side until we got to the emergency unit in Altnagelvin hospital, where hospital staff took over.

When people were injured in road accidents and fires, we had an interest in how they were progressing. We heard that the young woman lived for five days but unfortunately died from her injuries. I spoke to staff at the hospital and someone told me that it was nearly a blessing for her because her injuries were such that she would have suffered in a very bad way had she survived. I remember some people saying to me that she got all that she deserved – she was going to deliver letter bombs that were going to injure someone somewhere else. I accept that was the case but whenever I was dealing with it, to me she was just a young woman crying for her mammy.

That was a really bad experience. At the time I was a very young fireman – I wasn't a hardened person seeing this. The worst I would have seen before then was dressing a wound when I was nursing – nothing compared to what I met on that day. It really affected me. In the fire brigade at night, if there are no calls, you're allowed to go to bed and the boys said that for months after it I was having nightmares. In those days you were permitted to go to bed after eleven and I would normally have wandered off, but for months after that incident I never went to the dormitory on my own because, when I looked out of the dormitory window, I could see the building where all of this had happened. It had a very severe impact on me. I'm talking about something that happened forty years ago, and I still get upset. It's embarrassing and I try not to talk to a lot of people about it because I know that somewhere along the line I will get upset.

Aubrey experienced the aftermath of two more bombings in the city not long after.

One evening, fairly fresh in my time in the Fire Brigade, we were on night duty and got a call to Ebrington Barracks. I believe it was to the sergeant's quarters. When we arrived we were escorted to the building where the incident had happened. Someone had got into the building and planted a bomb beneath this soldier's bed. The bomb had exploded and, when we got there, the individual was dead. We were given the task of removing the remains from the bed, but such was the impact of the explosion that the wire springs in the bed had actually gone into the man's body. We had to get bolt cutters and cut away the remains of the bed springs in order to remove him. On this occasion the individual was dead, so it didn't have the same impact as the previous incident but it was fairly horrendous for the crews involved.

Another occasion, Muhammad Ali was due to fight. It was one of his big fights, and in Northland Station we were all settled down to watch it. It was about to start, maybe the bell had gone, when we all heard an explosion. There were a few expletives because we knew we weren't going to see the fight. At the time, we had the old Dennis fire engine. We got the call to Strand Road. We would have gone down Lawrence Hill so it was really a short distance to the incident, which was at a filling station – Maxol, I think it was. There was a car on fire beside a petrol pump. I believe the roof was missing off it. Myself and another guy, we jumped out and got the hose reels and we were fighting the fire when Station Officer Robert Cleary arrived. Suddenly Robert shouted, 'Stop!' and then said, through the smoke and the steam, 'Is that a body in there?' When we looked further, there was indeed a body in the back seat of the car.

It turned out it was a bomb that was being taken to wherever, and they had stopped to get petrol. There's something laughable about that if the whole thing wasn't so serious, get the petrol first and then do your dastardly deed.

But, as it turned out, the driver of the car and the pump attendant had been standing beside the car, as you would have done in the days when someone filled your car for you, and when they set the mechanism off on the pump, it set off the bomb. The guy we believe was holding the bomb on his knee had been killed. It was horrendous. There was a colleague of mine, Dessie Stokes – he and I joined together – and he was given the task of removing the body because he was wearing new gloves. A horrendous sight to see, as you can well imagine, when a bomb had gone off in someone's lap. There was a severe fire burning by the time we got there, so whatever the bomb hadn't destroyed, the fire had. The driver, who was one of the terrorists, had run away, but the pump attendant was still there and there wasn't a scratch or a burn on him. Evidently, the explosion had gone up rather than out because it had taken the roof of the car.

The frequency of large explosions, fires and incidents that led to loss of life almost overwhelmed emergency responders – and the local and national journalists who were covering the Troubles. As a result, there were many incidents that – because tragedy was averted – barely got coverage. However, for those involved, these were every bit as traumatic as those that got the headlines.

In the latter part of my service, a couple of years before my retirement, I was on night duty when we got a fire call. We didn't get any more information other than a particular address. It was within the estate where I live. When we arrived, there were people in the street frantically screaming, telling us that there were people in the house. Four people lived in the house but no one could tell us if there were three or four people inside. We were waiting on a pump coming from Northland, but we immediately took action and rescued three adults – an elderly lady and her son and daughter – from the house. It turned out that the fourth person had been out for the evening and wasn't home yet. The house was heavily smoke-logged. We got the mother and the daughter out and then discovered that the son – a man of around sixty-ish – was sitting out on a first-floor windowsill at the rear of the house.

I was the officer in charge and I had a crew of four with me. I got the driver – who was supplying the water for those who were going in – to go and get a couple of policemen and get a ladder off and go round to the back of the house. But by that time the Northland appliance had arrived and, instead of bringing the man down a ladder, they were able to bring him down through the house – by that time the smoke had eased.

Unfortunately the fire had been caused by people who had put flammable liquid through the letterbox and set it alight. The estate here would mainly be Protestant people – years ago it would have been more mixed, but the occupants were Catholics and this must have been the thinking of those who set the house on fire. They were apprehended fairly quickly as they had gone to a local petrol station and bought petrol. Eventually it went to court – one admitted his guilt and was sentenced accordingly but the other denied it and there was a court case we all had to attend. Fortunately the three occupants, whilst they had taken some smoke, did survive and recover. A very close call indeed. The younger lady, the daughter, actually got in contact with the Watch, and insisted that the crew come to her house and have afternoon tea. Which was a bit of a strange situation, but it meant that I was able to introduce the crew and say, 'Him and him were the two guys that carried you down; him and him carried your mother.' A happy ending to an awful situation.

One thing we did pride ourselves on down the years: we served all, favoured none. When you went out on a call, it didn't matter what colour or creed or religion you were, you had to rely on one another – it's that kind of job.

In the mid-1990s, the stand-off in Drumcree in Portadown caused widespread violence across Northern Ireland.

At the start of the Drumcree problems, I was again on night duty. It was a Sunday, if I remember rightly, and we were running all over the place to cars on fire and such. We were being directed from one call to another and then suddenly we were redirected to a car burning just up the street from where I live. My wife and younger daughter were still at home at the time and I said to the guys to pull in to a car park nearby until I assessed the situation because my wife and child were in the house. I said to the guys to put on their flash hoods, like the racing drivers wear, and to keep them well up. And I said, 'That's my house, so when we get there, no identifying who the crew are.' We had a situation where there were people there who didn't want the fire put out. One reason not to identify anyone. So we pulled up – of course there was one lady who was barging, 'What the hell kept you?' and all that. One of the crew members jumps out and the first thing he says is, 'Aubrey, will I put a hose reel on this?' So my talk about not identifying me didn't work. No hassle came to our house – although I'd still have preferred him not to identify me.

Today we almost take it for granted that first responders will be provided with the emotional support and practical help they need. However, this is a relatively recent development and not one that was there during most of the Troubles.

In the early days of the Troubles, we didn't have a counselling service – it wasn't talked about then. We were all big roughy-toughy firemen and we always believed in the fire service that we counselled ourselves. We would have come back to the fire station after bombings, or maybe serious road traffic accidents, where you would have seen horrendous injuries, and everybody would have got round the table, made a pot of tea or a cup of coffee, and you would have possibly talked through what you had seen. I'm sure lots of people went off and took different experiences home with them. I mean I'm recounting now something that happened more than forty years ago, and it's still fresh in my memory.

I was heavily involved with the Fire Brigade Union. We were continuously trying to better the conditions for our members, and counselling was one of the things we did fight for and eventually achieved. One of the things you would have done as an officer in charge is to get your crew together. Maybe you had one guy or one gal who was sitting back quietly, not saying anything, and you would have talked to them individually: 'Are you all right? There's a service here, would you like to avail of it?' I've no doubt in the early days proper counselling should have been there, but conditions have improved, and today I would say that there's an even better counselling service within the brigade.

Omagh

In the earlier stages of the Troubles, violence was mainly confined to Belfast and Derry/Londonderry. Initially, few country towns experienced much civil unrest, but this changed quite quickly and local fire crews – along with police and ambulance personnel – soon found themselves dealing with incidents the like of which they had never seen before. Bomb explosions, in particular, became all too common. For Omagh's retained firefighters, this exposure to the carnage caused by a bomb was shocking. The nature of things also meant that even after their service, firefighters felt utterly compelled to help in whatever way they could when their neighbours were in desperate need.

Paddy McGowan
Served for twenty-five years in Omagh retained.
Everything was fine from 1966, and then everything started to happen in '69. The experiences we had here were bad

enough, and I wouldn't compare them with what was happening in Belfast or Derry, but for a retained station ... some of the incidents that happened here were absolutely awful. I witnessed all of them and then in 1998, when I had retired and gone, came the Omagh bomb. I was driving into the town when the bomb exploded so I saw at first hand what was happening and saw the people at their worst – the bodies at their worst. I was well known in the town and it was known that I was a fireman, so when that bomb exploded that particular day in Omagh, and I and others were the first on the scene because we were close by when it happened, people were saying to me, 'Do something! Do something!' At that stage we didn't have the fire brigade at the scene, we didn't have the ambulance service at the scene, we had absolutely nothing at all. But I was the district manager with Ulsterbus and I looked across the road and saw one of my buses – it couldn't get through with the debris and all the rest of it. There was no ambulance, and people were saying to me, 'What are we to do? What are we to do?' I said, 'They have to get to the hospital – put them on the bus.' So we filled two big buses and sent to the depot for another. Some people had lost limbs. An ambulance can take one or two people but we took, I think it was, eighty-six on the three buses.

That was when I had finished with the fire service, but I recall very well the first incident I went to as a firefighter during the Troubles. It was the very early seventies, not far from where I live. There was a hotel called the Knock-na-Moe Castle Hotel and there used to be dances there at weekends. At about two o'clock in the morning, on a cold, dry, frosty morning, we got a call to an incident at the hotel. It was classed as a '7/7', which was a bomb. We left the station with two appliances, and headquarters told us to be very careful.

It transpired that the bomb was underneath a car at the hotel. There had been five soldiers in the car when the bomb exploded and they were blown here, there and everywhere. This was my first incident with death on that scale. There was an area near the hotel with big oak trees on high ground and I remember quite well the bodies were in every place that you could imagine. It was the first time we had to use plastic bags to collect pieces of men – and I mean pieces of men – and that incident stayed with us. I'm sure that right across Northern Ireland there were plenty of other incidents worse than that, but for us, as a wee rural town with a quiet station, where everything was peaceful, we didn't have that type of incident. We had the general run of road traffic accidents, fires and all the rest of it, and in the summer time we had heath fires, that was all part of our work, but we were never trained for and never expected some of the scenes and incidents that would follow in the years ahead. We were the first on the scene and we had to pick up the pieces. An officer arrived, I don't know who he was, but he arrived on the scene and instructed us on what to do. Our men worked hard. Myself and others didn't sleep or eat for many days after that incident. There was worse to come, of course, but nobody believed that – we thought that it was the end of the world at that particular incident.

The years following, we witnessed many incidents of death at first hand. We had a police Land Rover going into a crater with a couple of police who were both killed. I and a crew of four men got a call to what's now known as the Ballygawley bus bombing in August 1988. We got the call to that – all we could do was put tarpaulins on the road, and lay the bodies of all those soldiers killed in that bomb on top.

After that, I was called to the army headquarters and they asked why I had instructed a couple of my men to search the field near to where the bombing was. We'd always been instructed to be careful about searching in fields due to the risk of secondary devices, booby-trap bombs and so on but we couldn't ignore the area behind the hedge in a field in case there were men maybe still living, maybe injured. Some men might have been thrown out of the bus and into the field. Unfortunately we didn't find anyone but the army understood the reason. It was some comfort to know that our efforts were appreciated and later, for the response to this incident and others, I was privileged to receive the MBE.

Walter Johnston
Also spent part of his career in Omagh.

When I was based in Omagh, there were a number of rocket attacks. One of them was on Fintona RUC Station. The IRA had a ceasefire over Christmas, ending at midnight on Boxing Day. I was in the house in Omagh and there was an almighty explosion, and this was ten miles from Fintona. The siren went off and I got called out to this rocket attack on the police station. They fired four rockets at the police station. Luckily there was nobody in it that night, but the police wouldn't turn out to it, probably suspecting it was a 'come-on'.

I arrived and people were sweeping up the glass from the broken windows, but I was worried about this car that was down a side street and that was nearly down on to its axles. I went on the radio to control and said, 'Check out this number' – and it belonged to somebody who lived fifty miles away. I tried to explain to people that they needed to get back and get away from the car because there could be a secondary device. They used to put a bomb on to the vehicle that had the rockets in it to explode later on too, so you never knew what to expect. We pushed people back by getting into a line across the street and literally forcing them back down the street. We were putting our own lives at risk – obviously the people in Fintona had never had bombs, so they didn't realise what the consequence of that was. I went home that night in a cold sweat thinking about what could have happened. For years afterwards I had dreams about it.

I went to another rocket attack in Carrickmore. It was a

Saturday afternoon and it was the day we were having the kids' Christmas party at the fire station with Santa Claus. In the middle of the whole thing, the siren went off and we were called to a rocket attack at Carrickmore Police Station and army base. I still remember to this day the children in the fire station crying – they were so scared by what was going on. I drove out but I didn't know where the police station was and everybody I stopped and asked wouldn't tell me – the blue light was going on the fire car roof and they wouldn't tell me. I assume they thought I might be police.

Firefighters attending a call on bonfire night, 1984.

THE NORTH-EAST

Antrim

Antrim is close enough to Belfast that the fire brigade resources there could, when needed, be sent to the city – but far enough away for the town's own crews to have to manage an incident on their own for some time before any support arrived for them. With its close proximity to the airport and the M2 motorway – as well as a number of larger industrial sites – its crews attended a wide variety of incidents and felt the impact of the Troubles, just like everybody else.

Although all the stories told in this book are either very directly Troubles-related or have some aspect that connects them to the challenges of that period, the following story is included because it says a lot about the service and what it requires of its personnel – and their partners.

Stevie Cunningham

Joined the retained service in Antrim in 1975 while working for the airport fire service at Aldergrove. He subsequently served for thirty years in Belfast.

I was working for the airport fire brigade in 1975 and a lot of the boys in it were also in the retained. Within about three months of me being there I was in the retained in Antrim. I was working with a fella in the airport called Eamonn Kearney – he was a leading firefighter in the airport and he sort of took me under his wing. Eamonn was also a leading firefighter in Antrim retained.

The next year, 1976, on 26 May, I was in the house. We were living in Antrim, me and the wife, and she was expecting our first wee boy. I was in the middle of taking down the bannisters in the house when the bleeper went. I was one of the first ones down to the station because I was in the town. We had these small plastic tallies with our names on them that hung on a big board in the station. I grabbed mine and stuck it on the appliance crew board –that's what you did to put yourself on the truck. I saw the job was a lorry on fire on the Ballylurgan Road in Randalstown. So away we went. By the time we got there, this thing had been blazing for about half an hour. It was still blazing away. We turned around and pulled right up to the front of it. We got out and there was John Cochrane, one of the sub officers. Now John was a wee man, about four foot eight, with glasses, a country man, a nice man. Wee John was in charge. 'Right boys,' he says, 'take a hose reel up each side of it.' Now, there was no room up each side of it because each side of it was in the field. It was one of those road-lining lorries and at the front of it were all the gas cylinders. There were twelve gas cylinders on the front of the lorry, behind an angle iron guard.

There was all this paint sitting about and at the back of the lorry was the big boiler, where they boiled the paint – it's called chlorinated rubber paint, the paint that you melt. Below the boiler was a big gas ring. By law you're supposed to turn the ring off in between jobs, so that what went on to happen doesn't happen. I found out later that the guys were moving from one job to another along this wee road and they didn't turn off the ring – the paint started to slop over the top of the boiler, down on to the gas ring, and the paint went on fire.

Wee John says to me, 'Put the water on the gas cylinders.' Now I was about six, maybe seven, feet from the cylinders; just standing there, spraying the water. I turned to speak to the fella beside me and … I woke up ten days later.

I had done what they call spot cooling. Instead of spraying the cylinders, I must have put a jet of water under one of them. The bit of metal on the cylinder contracted quickly and all twelve of the things erupted. My wife heard the explosion in Antrim, although she thought nothing of it. The angle iron that was holding all the cylinders in place came straight out and wrapped around my face and down I went. The paint went everywhere and two or three other guys were covered in burning paint. They went running up the field with their hair burning, all the other boys running after them, beating them to get the fire out. A lot of mayhem. Then somebody realised, where's the big lad? Looking around they couldn't see me. I had landed in the drills for the potatoes; I was lying down there. They came over to me and decided that I was dead. One of the boys took his tunic off and laid it over me. Now, Eamonn Kearney, he was a Christian fella, and I think, to be honest, he may have given me the Last Rites, no matter where I came from. Eamonn heard me gurgling, air still coming out of me, so the next thing you know, he had the tunic off me, then he lay down on his back and got me on top of him, and he was pulling all the crap out of my mouth. I started breathing again. They sent for a helicopter and an ambulance. Two ambulances came first and they decided not to wait on the helicopter. Eamonn went with me and the ambulanceman to the City Hospital in the first ambulance and a couple of our guys went in the other ambulance. I was in a terrible bad state.

In between times, Tommy Evert, being the DO, and Bobby Bradford came to our house and rapped the door.

Marian, Stevie's wife, remembers the knock at the door.
I opened the door, and I was five months pregnant at the time, and one of them said, 'Did your husband go to a fire today?' and I said, 'Yes.' And he said, 'Well, there's been a bit of an accident,' and I said, 'Right, okay.' In those days I was very laid back and would never have thought of anything bad. He said, 'It's just protocol when a fireman is hurt on duty that we come and take the wives or parents to the hospital.' I said, 'Is he badly hurt?' and he said, 'Well, he's been cut about the face a bit,' and I said, 'Oh right.' So he said, 'If you would go upstairs and get ready.'

I went up the stairs to get ready because I had been cleaning. When I got down, they'd taken all the plugs out and the TV plug out and closed the windows. They brought me to the City Hospital and when I went in, there was Eamonn and some of the other firemen sitting. They were all covered in blood and dirt and whatever. I said hello to every one of them, still never thinking that something major could be wrong. The nurse brought me into a room and told me to put on a gown and a mask and a hat and these shoes that you put on before you go into theatre. When we got to the theatre door, this surgeon came out. He looked at me and he looked at the nurse, then he took the nurse to one side and said something to her. So the nurse took me back into the room, and said that Mr Phillips would be in to see me.

That was May – I was twenty-one. I was going to be twenty-two in August, and I was due in October. The surgeon came in and introduced himself and then said, 'Now, Mrs Cunningham, your husband's had a bad accident. He's in theatre at the minute. The Stephen that you knew will not be the same Stephen when you see him again.' Now, I thought the fire officers told me that he'd been hurt about the face. I said, 'Oh, is he going to be badly scarred?' He looked me in the face and said to me, 'Wait till I tell you, dear, when your husband comes out after all these hours of surgery – if he comes out – your guess is as good as mine as to whether he'll make it or not.' I said, 'Okay,' or some stupid thing like that. He says, 'If or when he comes out, he'll be transferred to the Ulster Hospital, so I advise you now to go home and ring them to see when or if he arrives.'

The nurse took me back out, and the fire officers asked me where I would like to go. Bear in mind, our families all lived in Belfast at the time. I thought it only right to go to his mummy and daddy so I asked the fire officer to take me to their house. When we got there – it was a wee kitchen house with a hall – the *Belfast Telegraph* was lying in the hall. I lifted the *Telegraph* and walked in and the fire officers came with me and I told his mummy and daddy what had happened. And it's as well I did, because when his daddy started reading the *Telegraph*, the story was in it – a twenty-one-year-old Antrim fireman had been badly hurt in an accident, with his wife expecting their first baby.

That was it until they told us that he had arrived at the Ulster Hospital. We went up to the Ulster Hospital. He was in intensive care. When we went in, there were two wee wards, and he was in the one next to the nurses' station. The doctors and nurses were messing about with this, that and the other. I think when I'd gone to the City Hospital with the officers, they thought he wasn't going to live. I went in every day to the Ulster Hospital, twice a day, with his mummy and daddy but, after the first day, I couldn't go in again for about three days. His head was the size of a pillow.

They told me that first night that once he got over twenty-four hours, there was a good chance he would make it. And then the next day, they said he would probably make it but that he was going to be in a vegetative state. And then the third day I went up they told me that his brain seemed to be okay. One night they couldn't get him settled and he was making all these sounds. They had discovered that he actually wanted a pillow – they had him lying flat and he always liked to sleep on a whole lot of pillows. That was a sign that the brain function was there. Then they said he was going to be blind. And he was, he was blind in one eye for a few months.

The extent and severity of his injuries was acute and the emotional impact severe, as Stevie relates.
I get emotional when I start talking about what was wrong with me. I had all the back of my hair burnt off. I burnt my head. I broke my nose. I broke my jaw in six places. I lost the roof of my mouth and most of my teeth. I fractured my skull. I had a tracheotomy, and had my own machine. I had an ear sort of chopped off, the bottom of it. Broken ribs, a broken arm. When I woke up ten days later, the dirt of the field was still on my pillow. And there they were telling Marian that I had a couple of cuts on my face.

Marian has reflected many times on why the senior officers weren't more direct with her about the seriousness of Stevie's injuries.

I think they may have told me a wee bit more if I hadn't been pregnant. They had him to deal with – they didn't want me going into premature labour. I honestly believe that if I hadn't have been pregnant, they might have told me a bit more.

You know the way some people nowadays have counsellors? In those days, forty-three years ago, nobody came. His friends out of the fire service and some of the officers came to visit him once he'd got out of the hospital. The accident happened on 26 May and, with all his injuries, they told me that I wouldn't see him out that side of Christmas. But he was out of hospital in three weeks and back to work in three months.

He tortured them to get out but he also tortured me when he got out because he didn't have the strength to walk up and down stairs or get dressed. All the guys came to see him and thought he was okay. They came one night and they were talking about his accident, the guys who were with him when it happened, and he got up and walked out of the room. I sort of looked round thinking, what do I do here? I went up the stairs to see, I thought he had maybe gone to the bathroom, but he was away ages. When I went up, he was sitting, crying his eyes out about the accident.

A few weeks after that the guys from the station were telling us about how bad he was, and he was thinking if he was that bad, how had they let him out of hospital so soon. And then he thought they'd let him out of hospital to die. I couldn't convince him otherwise. I had to get up one night, about two days later – I couldn't drive and I was six months pregnant by then – and get him to take me to the Massereene Hospital in Antrim to speak to a doctor. Even though it was about half two in the morning, they got me a doctor and I explained what was going on. I thought, I need somebody to speak to him now – he was starting to lose it and he was doing my head in. But they got a doctor in – they remembered the accident – and the hospitals, they had been on standby for casualties at the time. So the doctor came and spoke to him to try to calm him down.

As I said to him often, years later, they talk about counsellors and counselling and post-traumatic stress: no one ever came near us. That just wasn't the done thing in those days. Now the guys from the station came to visit and they did a collection moneywise, but nobody ever said to me, 'Are you okay?' I accepted that because in those days you got on with it.

We were young, we'd been fifteen when the Troubles first started and we'd been together then. We were living in the Troubles in North Belfast. I think that because of all your experiences then too, things like that don't tend to hit you until years later. Although, in saying that, maybe nowadays when you get counselling, those things don't hit you until later either. It wasn't until many, many, many years later that, when I thought of it, I could have cried.

Perhaps surprisingly, the brutal experience of the explosion and the life-changing injuries it caused didn't put Stevie off firefighting and less than a year later he had joined the full-time service.

Of all the things I've done and seen, the one that sticks in my mind was my first breathing apparatus job in Central. It was with Gordon McKee. We were called out to Canterbury Street at four in the morning, and we were in one of those stupid old fire engines from years ago, sitting backwards. I remember Joe, as we turned into the street, saying, 'Jesus Christ.' And I remember thinking to myself, fuck, what did he see? I looked round and on the middle floor of this house the flames were coming out, licking out. We arrived at the door and there was a bit of a crowd out – they were all half drunk. As I was putting the BA mask on, there was a wee girl on the top floor, up in the attic, and we could hear her scream. She was above the fire. I remember her yelling, yelling, yelling.

Me and him, we whipped up the stairs. Let me tell you, the heat was horrendous. There was a big stained-glass window on the landing, and Gordon put his hand through it – he ripped his hand to bits but we didn't know that. And we had to put the fire out to get past and get up to her. Jimmy Mason was the third BA man – there weren't even four of us – and we all blattered into the attic and the door closed behind us. I put my hand down and found her on the floor – she was dead. She was eighteen; a Dutch student. We got a hold of her and I remember going backwards but we couldn't get out, we couldn't find the door. And we were stuck in this attic with the wee girl.

We finally got her out and got her down to where the fire had been. The boys had put it out by then. The officer was, I think, Twiggy and he sent me and Gordon back up again. I could have cried. We'd to go back up in case there was someone else in there. I remember getting back up into that room. It was pitch black. I opened up the skylight. We searched right round the room. God help her, that wee girl sticks in my mind because she was the first person that I saw die in a fire.

Life has strange ways of making us reflect on experiences and a fire-call years after the Antrim explosion caused Stevie to think about the ways in which we break terrible news.

We got a call to the very top house on Alliance Avenue. We arrived at the door. The sun was shining; there was smoke coming out of this house. Anyway, I got into the garden. There was a wee woman lying there. A wee woman of about ninety, a frail wee woman, lying in the garden. The downstairs had caught on fire and the smoke was coming up. She'd got herself out one of those wee windows on the top floor and fallen into the garden. Now, this is one of the stupidest things I've ever done in my life: I'm up the stairs, ventilating, and poking about and the phone's ringing and ringing and ringing. By this time, the boys had her out over the garden wall. And this phone was ringing and ringing. It rang so much that I lifted it.

'Mummy, Mummy, are you all right?' And here's me, oh fuck me. I knew that the woman was in a very bad way and, in fact, she did die. I nearly put the phone down again. I said, 'Now don't panic. I'm a fireman, your mummy's had a wee bit of a house fire.' I was doing more or less the same thing they had done to Marian, playing it all down. And then she started squealing, and I just said, 'Well, you better get over here if you can.' Even for me to say the words, your mummy's dead. Dead's a big fucking awful empty word. Down with the phone and never again. It made me think about how the officers had told Marian so little about how badly I was hurt and how I sort of did the same with that wee girl about her poor mum. I suppose I'm a bit less hard on them now.

Ballymoney

Situated in the middle of County Antrim, Ballymoney is a well-established county town. It was largely – though not completely – spared the destruction that was visited upon so many other towns, and it rarely had any other manifestations of civil unrest. A quiet place that rarely made the headlines, it nonetheless suffered very painfully long after the most intense violence appeared to ebb.

Charlie McAuley
Joined the full-time service in 1978.
I served in Belfast right across the stations from when I joined in August 1978 up to March 1995. I had a number of promotions inside that time and I was at the rank of station officer. A job came up in a rural area in Ballymoney. I'm originally from north Antrim and I thought, this is an ideal opportunity to try to get back to where I came from. My

parents were still alive and lived on the farm and my brothers still owned farms in that direction, so I thought that's an ideal way to go. I applied for and got the job as the local fire officer in the Ballymoney area in March 1995. I spent a lot of time up there – in fact I stayed in that area until I retired in 2012.

There were a number of notable incidents during my time up there. One particularly difficult incident was in July 1998, on the eleventh night into the twelfth morning. I'd been on duty that weekend. As the local fire officer, on that night you expect to get a number of calls to various types of incidents mainly around and associated with bonfires, like fire spread and heat impinging on nearby premises. The first call came in at about ten o'clock, and I went to that and then several other calls in Garvagh, Coleraine and Ballymena. It was a busy evening up to maybe about two or three in the morning, when the last of the calls I had dealt with were finished. I came home and I thought, 'That's it now, it's quietened down so I'll go to bed.'

I was about ready to get into bed when my pager went off and it said, 'Turn out to petrol bomb attack, Carnany Estate, Ballymoney.' I was living in Ballymoney at the time and I knew exactly where that was, so I got dressed but just before I left, the phone rang and it was our control room. They said to treat this as 'persons reported. We have had several calls to say the house is well alight.' I got into the car. I knew where the engines would be coming from – I could actually hear them in the distance – so I drove out to where I knew I could rendezvous with them. They had obviously got the same information and as they were coming they could see the smoke rising.

We pulled up to the little square at the top of the street and there were a number of people – maybe about ten people – who appeared to be arguing and fighting and shouting, and there were a number of police officers there trying to control them. It was obvious that there was a severe fire burning. I got out of the car, pulled on my fire tunic and my gloves and went to the front door with the fire crew. I arrived with two full crews – twelve firefighters on hand immediately. We could hear shouting – 'There's kids in the house.' One crew was deployed to the rear of the property because that was where the main fire was. Myself and the sub officer, we went to the front door, which was open. I think the police had made an attempt to get in and couldn't – beaten back by the heat and smoke. Two firefighters were already wearing breathing apparatus. They were right behind us and, taking a line of hose, they went in. We were told then that there were children upstairs, so the first two firefighters went in and up the stairs, another two I asked to get ready and put on breathing apparatus and they were doing that. Within a very short time – less than a couple of minutes – the first firefighters came back down with a child. They handed that child to me and I carried him up the street to where there was an ambulance waiting and I placed him inside. He was dead.

The second BA team had gone in and, when I arrived back down at the front door, they appeared down the stairs with another child and placed him in my arms. I carried him up the street and placed him beside his brother in the back of the ambulance and went back down to the door. Then the first breathing apparatus team who had gone in appeared with a third child and gave him to me and I carried him to the ambulance. They were also both dead.

We had been told there were four children in the house and the third BA team were then rigged in BA and sent in to search the house. Meantime the firefighters at the back had quelled the fire – they had hit it hard and it was out. We searched that house top to bottom and we couldn't find a fourth child. We later learnt that the fourth child hadn't stayed there – he had stayed with another relative. We extinguished the fire, completed the search and searched the adjacent properties. Nothing else was found. We handed the scene over to police, left and went back to the fire station. It's a very difficult scenario – to go with the intent and the aspiration of rescuing people; of getting to people to get them out and to a place of safety, but obviously we couldn't do that. The children were dead. They were all just wee primary school kids.

The firefighters in Ballymoney Fire Station had formed very close relationships. They'd had a serious tragedy themselves. A few years earlier at the fire station, a firefighter had lost his life, so they were a very close-knit group of individuals who served under the command of their local sub officer, Di Getty. He was a fantastic individual, a fantastic firefighter, and a very strong character in terms of being able to deal with any difficulties within the station.

When we left the scene and came back to the fire station the first things that had to be done were the mundane jobs – replenish the engine, BAs, etc. I arranged with our welfare officer for counselling for any firefighters if they felt it necessary but I think the main thing was that comradeship, that camaraderie that we had as a group – we could talk to each other and be open and honest with each other. We did that and we went on with getting ourselves ready for the next fire call. These were all part-time firefighters – retained firefighters – and they lived and worked in the community, so once a fire call was over and done with they went back to their own homes, back to their own jobs and carried on with their own lives. But I felt that particular morning that I needed to speak to them all individually, make sure everybody was okay, and collectively we sat down together – we had a cuppa before everybody left the station. I also arranged for the welfare officer to speak to all of them individually, those immediately engaged in the incident.

There were so many instances where innocents lost lives and that is just an indictment of our society – that we put up with this for so long, for so many years. I thought about that incident recently and, while it impacted on me terribly, that pales into insignificance compared to the impact it must have had on that mother, or on the brother that survived because he hadn't been in the house. Those little kids would be in their twenties or thirties now, could very well have been parents themselves. I just can't comprehend how the family dealt with that. I remember the funerals, with the three wee white coffins being carried through the street in Ballymoney, and that just wrecks me.

Central Fire Station on Chichester Street, Belfast, after a bomb attack on the nearby Royal Courts of Justice in 1989.

BELFAST

Before the Troubles, the Protestant and Catholic communities were largely integrated. Things changed very rapidly when the Troubles erupted. While the affluent parts of the city and its suburbs were relatively untouched, working-class areas suffered massively from the ensuing violence and civil unrest – and the two communities quickly became separate. In subsequent years these areas became more and more divided and the death and destruction that characterised this period was at its most acute there.

Belfast had some of the biggest industrial and commercial buildings in Northern Ireland, and these were often targeted with bombs and incendiaries, resulting in huge, extremely challenging blazes and giving the expression 'the big smoke' a certain edge. While the most catastrophic impact of the Troubles was human loss, there was massive economic damage, with commercial property in the city centre targeted almost daily. In 1972, as the violence increased, the city centre was fenced off behind security gates. It was only possible to enter via these gates, where you were searched by military and civilian personnel. Commercial vehicles were also searched. This almost certainly reduced the number and severity of attacks but did not prevent them all – and before these precautions were put in place, a large number of bombs had been detonated with appalling consequences.

Firefighters faced the bombs, incendiaries and riots with a matter-of-fact stoicism. There was a direct impact on the service too with, for example, Central Fire Station on Chichester Street being seriously damaged on a number of occasions by nearby bombs, and being used on one occasion to launch an attack on the nearby police station. It eventually had bulletproof glass installed because it was being struck by gunfire directed at the nearby courts and security posts.

While the fire brigade's neutrality was largely respected and acknowledged, it wasn't universally so. When tensions were especially high, firefighters were often on the receiving end of violence that, whilst more often than not unplanned, was no less severe for that. It was certainly a very distinctive place to serve.

Desy Moynes

Was not long in the retained service in Armagh when he first visited Central Fire Station in Belfast.

Since I was a kid I followed the local retained guys in Armagh. Back in those days there was no pager – the siren used to go off in the town and as soon as you heard it you ran to the fire station to watch the fire engines going out. I always wanted to be a full-time fireman – that was my goal. I remember sometime early in '76 the old sub officer in Armagh, a man called Tony Crilly, had to go to Belfast on business. He happened to say to myself and John Nichol, another retained firefighter in Armagh, 'Do you want to come to Belfast?' Back in those days you didn't go to Belfast for pleasure; it was business you went for. He said, 'I'm going to park the car in Chichester Street Fire Station.' So the two of us went with him.

I remember going into the station and I'd never seen anything like it: huge fire station, five appliance bays along the front. We walked into it and John and Tony went on into the duty office to leave in the car keys and report who he was. I just stood in the station and this overwhelming smell hit me. It was just the smell of burning and the fire engines. I'd never seen fire engines like them. In the retained back in those days, there were the small Dennis fire engines and they were spotlessly clean and everything was kept where it was supposed to be – nothing was out of place. But in Belfast they were big working diesel fire engines, battered stupid from the riots with stones ... but just the overwhelming smell of smoke and the way the firefighting kit was just sitting at the back of it, I remember standing there looking at it going, 'I have to get here – there's no ifs or buts about it.' I applied for it and got it, and six months later I'd started my basic training. The following May I got my dream and I was in Central Fire Station on Chichester Street. I was on White Watch – I'd argue the best firefighting watch in Belfast. There are those who would disagree with me, but I'd argue, the best. And twenty-eight years ... brilliant, best job in the world.

Serving in the centre of Belfast – brilliant. It was a sort of organised chaos, if you could describe it like that. I mean the city was not like it is now – the city shut down at six o'clock in the evening and it became a ghost town. Nobody was out and about then. There was a feeling about it – you nearly knew something was going to happen. We used to take bets in the station at night about what time the alarms were going to go off in the buildings because at about one or two in the morning the incendiaries started going off in the shops and you could hear the sprinkler gongs starting. When the sprinklers went off they started a flow of water inside the building, but on the outside of the building there was a rotary gong that sounded to raise the alarm – so you often would have heard it about two o'clock in the morning. In the full-time stations you had dormitories and the gong would wake you – summer nights you would have heard the ding, ding, ding, ding and it starting to rotate and you were out of bed even before the call came in. When you turned out into Chichester Street and you looked back towards the city you could see the smoke swirling around the street lights. Some people would say I was mad to think this – but it was magic. Everything was a buzz and you'd just go and everybody got stuck in. I suppose, because of the watch, it was like a family. You trained together and worked together and everybody knew each other's job and there was none of this being told what to do when you pulled up at a fire – nobody needed to be told to do anything. It was like clockwork. We all knew each other's roles and whatever position you were riding in the fire engine that day or that night, there was a job nominated for that and you knew exactly what you had to do. Magic to us, you know.

You always had a bit of ... I'll not say a fear because the adrenalin was going – but sometimes when you got there and you looked at it, you thought, this is a bit iffy. But the guys who were in charge of me were all knowledgeable guys, they had come up before me in the worst of the Troubles, so I put my trust in them. They were good firefighters. If someone said to you that at some time they weren't afraid, well, to me they just weren't there, because if you weren't afraid, you were crazy. I mean you wouldn't want to let your colleagues down either, so everybody just worked together as a team.

Bobby Pollock

Joined the full-time service in 1966, having served in the British Army.
In the fire service, things were based on naval tradition. In the old days, when you had fires, the best people to go up the old rickety ladders and go across the rooftops were ex-navy men, because they were used to the rigging on ships. So when the navy men didn't want to go to sea any more or retired, they would become firefighters in the old Belfast Fire Brigade. All the naval terms the firefighters used came from them: you didn't have a kitchen, you had a galley; you had the mess, where the people you served with on duty would put their money together and buy food – that would be your mess ... you would eat in your mess. You had dormitories, dorms, and bunks, though it was all single beds. All naval terms. When you talked, you didn't talk about rope, you talked about lines; when you saluted somebody, you saluted in the naval tradition – you didn't stamp your feet, you put your feet together smartly.

When I joined in 1966, the fire service was a civilian fire service, in the sense that it dealt with chimney fires, small fires in houses and cars on fire, stuff like that. In the brigade, people would say to you, go into the job, do ten years, then look for promotion, because it was a very small brigade. As people retired, other people were promoted – there was no big influx or anything like that.

In 1969 everything erupted. When the Troubles started, everything changed. What saved the Belfast Fire Brigade, as far as I'm concerned, was the number of men who were ex-service, who had gone through the war, who had experienced the bombings and stuff like that. They helped the younger ones, like I was at that time. They held us together and made sure that we were able to cope with what went on, because there was no counselling and there was no advice given. The older hands looked after the younger ones.

The first bombs that came were a big shock to everybody – nobody thought that that would happen. Most of us had never heard a big explosion before, but as I said, the older hands, the ones who had served in the army and Dunkirk, Normandy, they had seen all this before, they were able to steady us, to make sure that we carried out our duties and our duty was to put out the fire. We never took sides. We did exactly what we were told to do – put out fires and rescue people. Save life, save property and then save yourself – that was the three things we used to do. It was scary in the sense that it was new to you, but it was exhilarating and you learned an awful lot very quickly.

As bomb attacks became more frequent, casualties increased. On 4 March 1972 a bomb detonated without warning inside the Abercorn Bar. The number of victims and the severity of their injuries came as a shock to the public and to the responders.

I was on White Watch and it was a Saturday. It used to be a routine on a Saturday that you came on duty, you did your drills, your equipment checks, and then you would go for a lecture. Once it was over, you would come down and get your kit cleaned – everybody cleaned their boots, cleaned their large belt, made sure their helmet was polished up and any equipment that needed cleaned on the machines was done, and then you would go and have lunch. I think it was just after lunch that we got the call – we heard the bomb go off because we were in Chichester Street. We heard a loud explosion and we got on the appliances and went round to it. When we got there, there was a lot of smoke and debris lying about Castle Place. There was a lot of police and army running about. There was a bit of a fire at the back of the building so the likes of myself ran out hose, the officers assessed the situation, the drivers made sure we had water getting into the pumps. Then we went in and we started to find bodies, people lying across a table, under tables. The strange thing to me about the Abercorn was that, although it was a big bomb, there was very little blood. I believe that was because, when the bomb went off it shattered all the glass – there was glass in the building and it cut people to pieces – but the heat sealed the wounds so there was very little blood. We carried people out: there was a lady with a large table leg through her thigh; there was one girl we laid out, whose eye had been cut in half by flying glass.

I had gone in with a guy called Lloyd Brown, a good firefighter, and we found a chap who had lost both his feet. We picked him up and carried him outside. The ambulance was there but there was no room on any of the beds so we had to lay him on the floor. We went back in and found his feet and we wrapped them in an old bit of curtain or something and we set them in with him in the ambulance. He went on and then we went back in. We were looking at trying to get more people out. The scene started to calm down then and order came, the way it always does in an incident. For the first couple of minutes there is chaos and then everything gets into order and we deal with it.

That night we had planned to go to a party, all the firefighters on White Watch and their wives. We talked, we said, right, we'll still go but we won't talk about it. But of course as soon as we got to the house, there was talk about it. There was a fair amount of drink taken and the women were very – how could you put it? – they could understand, I think, the tension we had at that time. They were very helpful and tried to calm things down, drove us home and all the rest of it, because everybody had a right few drinks.

It used to be that if there was an incident and you came back, there was always some older hand would talk to you and he would say, 'Well, what did you think?' He'd tell you, this is why it happened – you weren't involved, you weren't to blame and anything you did, you did for the good of the people that you were helping. Now the sights you still had in your mind, you couldn't erase them, but you were reminded that you were there helping people so anything you did was beneficial. Unfortunately at certain times, there are little things that trigger it, and it comes just like a flash, then it goes away again … but it's something we've learned to deal with and, thank goodness, now there are a lot better mechanisms in place to help people through bad experiences.

In the earliest years of the Troubles, bombs and incendiaries were planted first and foremost to kill, maim or damage their principal target. However, over time this tactic evolved and in many instances, the intention was to draw the security forces in to attack them more effectively. In situations when terrorists targeted commercial premises, the tendency for firefighters was to immediately rush in to try to save a building but this was clearly not what the attackers wanted to happen, so secondary devices were often left to 'discourage' this.

In the earlier part of the Troubles, we never worried about secondary devices until we got a call to College Square North, an electrical wholesalers in a big Georgian house. There was a row of them. A bomb had gone off. As we arrived up – a crew of five of us, I think there was – the army said there was a small fire at the back. We unrolled the hose and were pulling the hose through to put the fire out, but as we got through what was left of a window, the hose burst. So I went back to get a fresh line of hose, so that we could run it out. As I was running it out and coming through the window, there was a flash about eight to ten feet from me. It was a secondary bomb left to catch the firefighters. Now what saved us was that, when the first bomb went off, the detonator had blown upwards and brought down some heavy stuff that was on the floors above. The second one did the same thing, but there was a gap, so the blast went right through to the ceiling, right up into the rafters, so stairs and dirt and stuff like that had come down. We were all covered in muck and deafened because of the explosion. Guys who were further away, at the front, were jammed – they'd been blown over in between washing machines and whatever else there were, fridges and stuff like that.

I thought I had gone blind – I could see nothing – and I could hear nothing either. I put my hand down to check that I was in one piece, and then slowly I could hear buzzing as if my hearing was coming back. I could hear guys shouting, 'Is everybody okay? Are you okay?' The word went out from one of the leading firemen who'd arrived up: 'Send all the men and all the lorries,' meaning send more appliances because people are trapped. Not standard terminology, but the control room knew what he meant! I could see people coming through the crowd, through the rubble to help us. I didn't know who they were or what they were, but they grabbed hold of me and started to bring me out. We used to wear a really thick belt and I realised that, when the bomb had gone off, my body had sucked in and the belt had dropped to the floor. When I was moved, they found my belt intact and lying about four feet from where I was, so I don't understand what happened there.

We all got out and everybody was put into a minibus and taken up to the Royal Victoria Hospital. Everybody was checked out. We had a lot of glar and mud stuck in our throats, ears and eyes, but everybody got checked out and everybody was good. They said that they would have considered us lucky if we'd lost an arm or a leg, because we were so close to the blast, but the way the blast went, it didn't affect us. They sent men out to our houses to tell our wives that we'd been injured – that we were safe, but we had been injured. We came back into the station in the minibus, all black faces, red eyes. The senior officers walked us into the officers' mess and bought us all a brandy and were all sent home. There was guys who came back within two days, I was back within three days. Everybody returned to duty, nobody stayed off for any length of time. Our hearing had been affected, it was affected for a while, but nobody had any physical damage. I was fine until I got home and saw my two small children and I broke down and cried then. It was just one of those things that had happened, we survived it, so that was it. Yes, they told us that we were very lucky the way the bomb had gone off, but it was a deliberate act to kill firefighters and policemen.

The paramilitaries would never say there was a second bomb, but they had realised that we would go in quick. As a result they'd often leave other bombs, hoping we would wait for the army disposal to come, knowing that by the time the building was clear, the fire would have caught and the whole thing would be lost. So rather than do nothing, we used to go up as close as we could, put in the big ground monitors – these were hoses on stands that we could aim and then leave – and then just pour water into it. So that although we weren't in the building, the place was getting soaked.

They put a car bomb in Belfast city centre, further up the street from the Crown Bar, on the same side as the Europa. We arrived, we put tape across. As we were putting ground monitors down to cover the car, we could hear a lot of noise coming from the Crown. We thought there couldn't be anyone in there, because everyone should have been well back in case the car bomb went off. So myself and another guy went into the bar to see what was going on and the place was packed – they were all standing up against the tape and we said, 'You can't stand there – there's a bomb.' This fella says, 'No, no, the policeman says if we're this side of the tape we're okay.' They imagined that this was a magic wall that would have stopped the bomb. Thank goodness the bomb didn't go off. Bomb disposal guys, who always did a great job, were able to defuse it. We got it sorted out. And the drinkers weren't disturbed that much.

Alan Brown

Joined the retained service in Newtownards in 1957. In 1962 he joined the full-time service and was based in Central Fire Station in Belfast until he retired in 1987.

I saw my first bomb when I was in Red Watch. It was at the Wilson and Leeper showroom, which was at Bridge End. It was a big car showroom and the cars were blown out like Dinky Toys into the street. We had never seen anything like it. We were positioned two up and two down – two appliances up and two down – and we got a grandstand view.

On 21 July 1972 the IRA detonated twenty bombs across Belfast. The total number of people injured was around 130 and 9 people were killed.

I was on duty on Bloody Friday and I wouldn't relate some of the things I saw. The first call I went to that day was to the Cavehill Road shops – to the bomb that killed the Rev. Parker's son. We turned out with one appliance, the emergency tender, which I was driving. Sub Officer McCabe was in charge but on the way to that we were redirected back to Oxford Street, to the bus station. As we drove in I saw an item in the middle of Townhall Street. I thought it was a cat but it wasn't – it was a scalp, a black scalp in the middle of that street, which I drove over. I can see that scalp now in the middle of the street and I woke up at nights thinking about it and there was an ear on it ... There was no counselling ... at all.

One of the most financially costly attacks of the entire Troubles was at the Belfast Co-op on York Street on 10 May 1972. Probably the largest shop in the city, a number of bombs left inside started a huge fire that destroyed the building. Virtually every firefighter and fire engine in the city was sent and they made a heroic effort to save it. However, its modern design meant that the firefighting was complicated and extremely dangerous. Some of the firefighters well and truly put themselves in harm's way to try to save it.

We got a call to the Co-op in York Street. I was a turntable ladder driver and operator that particular day, driving the 100-foot Merryweather turntable ladder (TL). We came down and there was quite a bit of smoke about. I parked the appliance in front of the building, at the York Street end, because the turntable wasn't needed at that time. The fire had been started by incendiary bombs – little bombs placed in clothing or in carpets. The devices eventually ignited throughout the building so the inside of the place was burning. They were probably fighting it from the inside. After some time I was asked to take the ladder into Frederick Street, which was along the side of the Co-op. We noticed that the roof was starting to burn. Now the roof would have been covered with pitch, so there was more smoke than fire, and I was told to set the ladder in as a water tower – when you extend the ladder above the height of the building. There's a hose pipe taken up the ladder and that means you can pour a copious amount of water down on top of the fire to douse the flames. The water pressure at the bottom could be seventy or eighty pounds but was much less at the top.

While I was in the process of setting that up, somebody beside me on the ground drew my attention to two firemen on the roof of the building. This changed things. They hadn't their helmets on – they were waving the helmets over the edge of the building. Obviously they were trapped there – now I had to do something about that. I didn't have to be told to do it. I knew those two guys had to be brought down. I swung the ladder in but it couldn't get near them

– these ladders have limit stops and for safety reasons this cuts out the movement. You see, if you use the ladder as a water tower you position it so that, if the wall of the building collapses, it doesn't collapse on top of the appliance. So I was two-thirds of the way across Frederick Street for safety reasons and I couldn't get in to get near them. So I shortened the ladder and brought it down to about level with the roof. Now, normally when you're operating the TL, you bring it in absolutely steady; you don't swing it because there's a man at the top and it swings about.

This day I must have been working at seventy-five feet but I brought it in flying – rough, really rough. If I had been on a training course they would have put me down for it but I swung the head of the ladder over towards the building, and one of them, Leslie Johnston, jumped on to it. I personally couldn't have done it, but he jumped on to that ladder, and he shouted to me, 'Do it again, do it again.' I made the same rough movement and Leslie caught the other firefighter and pulled him in under the ladder so he was hanging below it, seventy feet off the ground. Now I wasn't sure if Leslie had one of his hands through the ladder or if his feet were on the round so I couldn't shorten the ladder – it would cut your hands or your fingers off and if his toes were in there they would have been cut off too.

So what could I do? I trained the ladder round more slowly across the street. On the other side of Frederick Street there was a bible bookshop. I took them to the top of that and there was a parapet wall on the front of it. A parapet wall is where the wall extends up above the roof line. One of them was able to drop off the ladder and land on the roof. Now I think, although I'm not sure, I think that Leslie was still on the ladder and he walked down when I lowered the ladder down. It was luck that I was able to swing the ladder in, and it was a bad movement, bad TL operating, but it worked. Apparently they still show that video in training to show what you shouldn't do with a TL – but it worked. We were at a lunch one day and I happened to be sitting beside Leslie Johnston. He put his arm around my neck and he lifted me up by the head, and said, 'This man saved my life.' I was more embarrassed than anything else.

I never thought about danger: we were going out to calls, I was in the fire brigade, I was expected to do this. No, I never worried about it. Once, though, I got an awful scare. The morning of internment, we got a call to the Macnaughton Blair premises, which were then off the lower Newtownards Road at the Albert Bridge. It was a steel building, actually it was the old building the buses were kept in, and again I was a TL operator. I had a man up the ladder, Fireman Billy Little, when the building collapsed. Now the sound of collapsing steel, I would describe it as like the shaking of a massive chain. The sound of that steel collapsing … and it threw red embers up toward where this fireman was. All I could do was to trail him away from it and get him down. That was the only time I can say I was scared: the noise of that and knowing I had a man up there who I couldn't leave. I would say that's the only time I was scared. You know we accepted it, we all accepted it – it was our job. You hear doctors crying out now about the work they're getting. They wanted to be doctors – take it. I wanted to be a fireman – I took it … Hope my doctor's not reading now.

Walter Johnston

Joined the full-time service in Belfast in 1974. Amongst the many bomb attacks and fires he attended, some particular incidents still bring back vivid memories, including one that resulted in an unusual use for the turntable ladder.

When I was stationed in Belfast there was a massive fire at Linfield's Cash and Carry. There were two or three bombs there – the fire started on the ground floor and went up through the building. We were fighting the fire – we'd two TLs set in and twenty pumps there. The building was a six-storey traditional warehouse, well alight, especially at one end. It was near Blythe Street, off Sandy Row. We were dealing with the fire when there was a partial collapse inside the building and we had fire crews inside. The officer in charge told me to go up the TL and find these boys and bring them down – to use the TL as an external stair. I ended up, by myself, walking along the top floor of that building, as far as I could go, and it was burning. The top floor must have been used for servicing gas meters because I remember all these gas meters lying about. I couldn't find any of the boys so I came down the TL and then had to move it. It turned out that the ones inside had been in the building but had come down the back staircase – and they were having a cup of tea. I couldn't find them because they had gone to get a cup of tea! But I remember that fire in Blythe Street mainly because we couldn't stop it. One minute it was a clear, nice sunny day, and the next you couldn't see two feet in front of you because of the black smoke.

There was a conveyor belt company in Blythe Street on fire as well – the fire had spread. But there was a steel door in the building between that and the Linfield Cash and Carry. The steel door was red hot, and we were inside trying to put that fire out. The amount of hose we had out and the actual intensity of that fire was just unbelievable. There was a lake or something on the other side of the railway line and we had to run hose across the railway line, running it underneath. We dug holes so the train wouldn't be stopped – we didn't use hose ramps, strangely enough. The next morning we went down on relief and the TL was there, and the people that owned the Cash and Carry said we could take the damaged stuff – it would be dumped anyway – so the TL was filled up with Tic Tacs.

A near miss that I still have dreams about was up at Ballysillan, at Wolf Hill Mill. It was a four-storey sandstone warehouse full of jute that got torched. One of the old hands, Jimmy Greeves, was there. There was this entry between the building that was on fire and the building beside it – a four-foot entry between the two. It was really wet, and I was so young and keen, and because the flames were coming out through the windows, I said to Jimmy about putting a jet into one of these windows. Jimmy said, 'Sure the building's lost.' So we ran a jet on down and at the end there was a large entrance into the warehouse. Another firefighter, Eddie Rollins, was standing there with that jet and about twenty minutes later there was a massive rumble and we ran. There was about three or four feet of sandstone on top of our jet. We went to go up the entry again and there was eight or ten feet of sandstone blocks in the entry, so if Jimmy had been as keen as I had been that night, we wouldn't be alive. Me being the youngster – I was only in the job a couple of years – and his experience … He knew there was no point. I still think about it the odd time. You couldn't have survived that – big blocks of sandstone coming down on top of you. The whole building just collapsed in on itself.

One Sunday night we got a call that a warehouse was on fire at Lawther & Harvey Transport, near Cupar Street, up on the Falls Road. It was a six-storey old traditional warehouse and the fire was out through the roof – all six floors burning. We arrived up but we had to wait because the soldiers were having a gun battle with the IRA inside the transport depot. They burnt something like thirty-odd lorries in the depot that night. We had to wait underneath this loading bay as the soldiers were still shooting at the boys inside the depot. I was running about looking for a fire hydrant and the army had all the lights out – they'd turned all the street lights out to protect themselves. I was running down the street with a standpipe bar and key and there was a soldier in a doorway but you couldn't see him until you were actually standing beside him – it was just totally pitch black. After the army said it was okay, we dealt with the warehouse fire, but by that stage the building was effectively lost. The rumour still goes about that there were people on the roof of that building firing at the army – they were never recovered if there was anybody there. It was said that there was a gunfight going on between the gunmen on the roof and the army when, for some reason, the roof caught fire. We went into the main office building at Lawther & Harvey's to put out a fire and there must have been a couple of hundred bullet holes in the glass doors and panels in the front foyer.

Most fires that followed bomb or incendiaries attacks were tackled with water, but some incidents required a different approach – and occasionally this involved producing huge quantities of foam using a specialised foam tender. For most firefighters this was a rare event and not something they were especially well practised in.

One day shift we got a call to a suspect device on an oil tanker outside Donegall Pass Police Station. We arrived down and the ammunition technical officer was there, so we sat at the bottom of the Lisburn Road, at Bradbury Place. The next thing, there was this almighty explosion. We looked around and all we could see was a big puff of white smoke coming up from the tanker – it had exploded. The lids from the top of the tanker ended up around the fire appliances near the ATO – which shows you how far the lids blew. We went in to put the fire out. Whitla Street's foam tender was there with its foam cannons and I was on a number ten branch – one of the big 'guns' for pouring on massive amounts of foam – putting the fire out on the tanker and trying to protect myself behind a give way sign. It looked a lot worse than it was, but there were about ten or fifteen cars on each side of the tanker, parked on the roadside, and whenever the tanker went off, the burning oil went underneath all those cars, so we had all these cars on each side of the tanker on fire too. The ground floor of the bank on Shaftesbury Square and all the ground floors of the buildings right along the side went on fire, including the police station. It was a big incident and it was the first time I'd ever used a number ten branch. The funny thing about that one was, I was putting the fire out and there was about two or three feet of foam in the street, and I said to somebody, 'God, I've lost my watch.' One of the other firefighters said, 'No, I have it.' I said, 'How did you find it?' and he said, 'I didn't. There's a soldier there who saw you drop it.' I'd had ideas of me getting out a squeegee and going through all this foam looking for my watch.

With us being in Cadogan Fire Station on the Lisburn Road, we were nearly always first in when they needed extra resources in the city centre. You'd be driving down into the city and there wouldn't be that many people about, and after 6 p.m. there wouldn't be two people on the streets – it was just a ghost town in those days. There were so many bomb and incendiary attacks, you couldn't even remember them all. One of the interesting ones was at the gas office and the tax office on Ormeau Avenue – two big six-storey buildings. Well, one Sunday night we got the gas offices – the IRA had put one of those 'hangers on' blast incendiaries on the ground floor, and on the grilles on the windows of Tyrone House opposite they'd hung two kit bags. They used bent clothes hangers to attach the bombs to the grilles. From their point of view, they worked a treat – the bomb went off, smashed the window and sent ignited petrol straight into the building. The bomb went off in the gas office building and the fire started on the ground floor but we couldn't do anything until the ATO cleared those two other bombs. We then stood for about an hour just watching the fire go along the ground floor, start to go up the staircase, then up on to the roof, then slowly but surely devour the building, dropping down floor by floor. We watched it for at least an hour from the building in the back.

When we did start to put the fire out, the coping stones – big sandstone coping stones from the windows on the top floor – fell out and landed close to us. These things weighed about half a ton each. A fire started on the roof of Tyrone House due to radiant heat so Jimmy Greeves and myself were put up to the wheeled escape ladder to deal with it. We were going up to the roof with a hose reel and we were almost to the top of the ladder when I said, 'Jimmy, this ladder is not "pawled"' [locked] and we were up full extension. When you put the ladder up you normally drop it down on to the pawls, but when we were up there, it was only being held by the brake on the handles. You've never seen two guys come down a ladder as quick in your life. Jimmy was up at the top and I was about six feet below him. We were a bit lucky that time.

I used to always go to Central on 'out-duty'. That's when they were short of men and someone was sent down from one of the other stations to make up the numbers. I was there one day and we got a call to Corry's timber yard down at the docks – that's the only time I ever saw the fire tug being used. The fire was in a massive warehouse. There were swinging doors into the warehouse and you knew it was a very serious fire because the wind it whipped up was pulling the doors closed. We had something like two TLs at that, plus the fire tug, and we must have used about twenty jets. They had wire grilles on the first-floor windows. We were trying to break the wire grilles with stones so we could break the windows. One of the owners of Corry's was there and he pulled out his gun and shot six bullets through the windows. It was one of the boys' last night and he was up on top of the TL, wondering what was going on, with this buck eejit shooting windows out with a gun. I don't know why they were there, but there were five-gallon tins of silver paint. All of those exploded, and we were absolutely covered from head to foot with silver paint and we couldn't go back to the fire. We'd to put paper down on the seats, and even the door handles were covered in silver paint. It took about two hours to clean my boots – everything in the fire engines, everything, was covered, as the paint had floated on the water that we were wading through at the fire. Absolute pain.

Dickie Sefton

Joined the full-time service in 1955 and served in Belfast for all of his career.

One of the first nights of the Troubles was in August 1969. Unknown to me, the fire brigade had been withdrawn, the police had been withdrawn. I didn't know and I came into the top end of the Falls Road and drove straight into a riot. Now in those days the fire cars were marked with 'Fire' and just had a blue flasher on the roof. They took me for a policeman and smashed the windscreen and threw in two petrol bombs. The car went out of control, and eventually crashed, but I was able to roll out. If I had've been wearing a seat belt, I wouldn't have got out. The chief officer, Billy White, was with me in the car. He was able to get out and he ran down the Falls Road with his head and his hands on fire. He was an older man and he died about a year or two later.

I heard these two voices, the first saying, 'That's not a policeman, that's a fireman,' and the other saying, 'Doesn't matter – let the bastard burn.' Then I heard somebody making strange noises and I didn't know then but I know now that it was a Mrs O'Rawe, who tried to beat out the flames on my face with her bare hands. I couldn't get any air cause the flames were taking the oxygen away from me. My hands were on fire too. I lay there for long enough before the ambulance arrived, I didn't lose consciousness. By this time the fire brigade had got through and they were able to take me to the hospital. My whole face is a skin graft – every bit of it is a skin graft.

That happened in August and I didn't go back to duty until February. And I was worried in case I didn't get my job back – I couldn't wait to go back into the fire brigade again because I missed it. I went through a medical and they said that, seeing I was a senior officer I could go back on, so I went back on duty.

I eventually got throat cancer and they removed my voice box – they had to remove that much of my throat to get it sorted. I've got an electric voice box now. I don't know if it's connected, but I had swallowed burning petrol and it was two weeks before I could speak … A long time after that I was told there were photographs of the attack – and I had to go to a certain place in a street near where I'd been attacked and buy them!

When I got back to fitness and back on duty, things were hectic. We were under a lot of pressure. One night one of the big timber yards in West Belfast got attacked and the whole place was burning. Heat from the timber yard was threatening some old people's bungalows nearby. In those days the barricades were up and they wouldn't let the army or the police through so we got a call to send up an officer to check the bungalows. I went up and these guys were searching me, and they said that I wasn't a fireman; I was an army intelligence officer. I said, 'Think what you want – I'm a fireman,' so they said, 'Right, you can bring in two fire engines but only for the bungalows – if we see you putting water on that timber yard, we will shoot the firemen.'

I went in with two fire appliances and we put out the fires in the bungalows. I went to put a message back to control and the radio handset was torn out … no radio. In the meantime, they contacted the fire brigade and told them we had to stop all the firefighting operations in the timber yard or they would shoot the firemen. Controls contacted us through one of the other appliance radios and we immediately suspended firefighting operations – the timber yard went up. They kept us there, then they let the two fire engines go but they kept me a while longer. When I was coming out they said to me, 'Your fire engine won't get very far because we have planted a bomb on board it,' and I had no radio because they had ripped it out. I had to go away down the Falls Road like a sprinter and stop the fire engines. We searched them – but there were no bombs on board!

Jimmy Armstrong

Joined the fire brigade in November 1965.

We were on duty the first day the Troubles really started
in Belfast. It was a Friday. The first call we got must have
been at about half three: I was driving the pump. I won't
mention the name of the sub officer who was in charge. We
got the call to Conway Street Mill, that we should go in via
Clonard Monastery. I says to him, 'There's no way Clonard
Monastery is near Conway Street Mill. We can't get in from
there.' He said, 'That's the call. You just go there.' And I says,
'Okay, but I'm telling you we can't get in.' When we pulled
up at the front of the monastery and the chaplain came out
– Father McLaughlin, who was a Derryman. He came out
and I said, 'Will you tell this man that Conway Street Mill
is nowhere near here?' 'That's right,' he says. So the sub says
to me, 'Do you know where it is then?' And I said, 'Aye,
sure we passed it on the way up the road.' Back down to
Conway Street. The fire was now going well: a bomb had
gone off in it or something. Anyway, we sorted the fire out,
we didn't go into it. Then a crowd came up the Falls Road,
must have been about a hundred men, and the sub officer
started panicking. I says, 'We're all right.' This man in the
crowd, I knew him, and he said, 'How are you, Seamus?'
And I said, 'I'm the best, what about yourself?' And he says,
'What's going on?' And I said, 'We need them windows
broke to get the water in through them.' So they broke the
windows for us.

Anyway, we had to leave because they said there was a gas
cylinder in it, a big tank, so we left anyway and were going
down the Falls Road, down Divis Street towards Dover
Street. This mob come out of Dover Street with death in
their eyes. And I said to the sub officer, 'Will you put them
horns on?'

'Oh, no, no, no–'

I says, 'Put the horns on until we get through that lot.'

And he said, 'No, no, no–'

And I put the horns on. I said, 'Them or us, but it's not going to be me,' and I drove through them. And that's the first escapade we had during the Troubles. I think the sub officer needed clean underpants and everything back at the station all right.

Bloody Friday in 1972, I was in fire prevention. It was busy. John Hyland, station officer, and I came across the first bomb. We were heading out to a fire safety inspection on the Holywood Road, a children's home, and we found a car abandoned on the Sydenham Bypass. So we radioed that through and came back and the place was chock-a-block. We couldn't get up along the bypass so I cut through Dee Street and down along Queen's Road and on through the harbour property. Then the bomb went off over near the Lifeboat Bar – it lifted the fire car off the ground.

We got back to the station and we were standing in the middle of the yard when the bomb went off in the bus station. That day was a very strange day. My mate George Gordon from Annalong – George and I were neighbours out in Carryduff and pals all our life in the fire brigade – was on the emergency tender and had been out for most of the day. When the bomb went off in the Oxford Street bus station, I think we waited fifteen minutes or more on a pump, then two arrived. There were new recruits in the yard and we got them, and we got the hose out of the hose store and a couple of standpipes and got the fire out. A bad, bad day.

We used the engine room as a casualty clearance station, and Captain Mitchell – who was the chief officer – came out at about five o'clock or half five and said to George Marshall, 'Leading fireman, will you lift that piece of paper off my engine room floor?' Now George Marshall told the chief officer where to go and what he thought of him, so he did. On the way back home to Carryduff I broke my Pioneer Pledge. I was a Pioneer. I didn't drink but George Gordon threw a half pint of vodka and Coke into me in the Ivanhoe Bar on the way home that night. That was the first time I'd ever had a drink, so it was. It was Gordon who put me on the drink.

There is no doubt that firefighters serving in Northern Ireland during the Troubles were experiencing things that rarely, if ever, happened to their GB or Irish colleagues. In part it was the scale of what they were dealing with as well as the sheer carnage they were exposed to, but there were also less conspicuous things – like being attacked and threatened. Jimmy had a particularly scary experience.

It was the last Friday of April in 1973, and it was the last Belfast Fire Brigade officers' mess dinner down at a hotel in Whiteabbey. I was there that Friday and about three o'clock they said to me, 'There's a call come in from Plevna Street on the Falls Road. A defective flue.' In those days, in the Belfast Fire Brigade, you had to go out to everything. There was nobody there in fire prevention so they gave me Big Slim, who was the water man, to accompany me. I couldn't tell you what his real name was. There was no spare car so Tommy Douglas, the divisional officer, gave me his. So we were in Plevna Street – I left Slim sitting in the car and I entered the house. As I was lighting a wee fire in the grate to see where the smoke is going, a boy burst in through the door with a gun and the gun was shaking. 'Right, get up, get up.'

'We're firemen,' I says, 'firefighters.'

'Out the fuck,' he says and put us into the back of a van and threw one of them auld bags that would have covered a fridge in transit, that type of thing, over us.

They took us to a derelict house somewhere. He said we were Special Branch, undercover officers, and fired shots behind our heads and our backs. He was one bad bastard, and he would have done the shooting and interviews. He had a Glens of Antrim, Larne-type accent. He still maintained we were Special Branch. I said, 'Go up to Ross's Mill and ask my father-in-law, Alex O'Hara. He'll tell you who I am.'

They went up to Ross's Mill, three of them, and got Alex

out. And of course the women in Ross's Mill saw what was happening and came out with the knives and stuff and they were going to do them, but Alex said, 'No, there's something wrong here.' So they asked him a whole lot of questions about me and the last thing they asked him was 'Does he speak funny?' And Alex said, 'To you and me he might, but he comes from outside Dungiven in north Derry, and he has a Donegal, Scots and Irish accent.' And your man turned round and said, 'You've just saved a man's life.'

They came back anyway and they were letting me go and they weren't going to let Big Slim go. I said I wasn't going without him and I told them I was an officer in the Fire Brigades Union and that if anything happened to Big Slim or anything like that, there would never be another fire engine in the Lower Falls and they could do whatever they wanted, I'd make sure there wasn't. They finally let us go.

We went back to headquarters in Chichester Street and I told the divisional officer about it and was taken up to the chief, Mr Mitchell. He looked at me and said, 'Something similar happened to me, you know, when I was in the army.'

I says, 'What?' I was standing in front of his desk and I was wound up to ninety, you know, to a hundred.

'In the army,' he says, 'I was taken prisoner.'

'Wait till I tell you, sir' I says. 'When you were in the army during the war you were protected by the Geneva Convention. Up the Falls Road they think that Geneva is a fucking bap out of Kennedy's bakery.'

He just turned and walked out and I very near told him where to go.

They didn't even have the decency to take me home – I didn't have a car at the time. God be good to Harry Moore, who worked in the fire prevention with us, he took me home in his car to Carryduff.

Alex, Mary's father, came over to our house in Carryduff that night. He asked me, 'Do you want to go for a walk?' I told him what had happened but Mary didn't know about it until a long time afterwards. The auld dolls up in Ross's Mill knew the boy that took us. He was one of the 'stickies'; the Official IRA – some time later he was shot dead at his home.

A few years after, I was in charge down in Central and we got a suspected five hundred pounder in Donegall Place, so the machines were parked in Donegall Square West. The way we did it then was we got the hose laid out and the ground monitor laid out and then the men went back into the appliances with the windows open so that, if the bomb went off, they had a bit of protection. That's the way we did it in Central anyway. We got the monitor all laid out and the boys got into the appliances, then I went up to the corner of Donegall Place to see what was going on. When I came back again to the machines the boys were all lined up against the buildings in Donegall Square West. I says, 'Right boys, what the fuck are yous playing at? Into your appliances. What are yous doing standing out here?' It turned out that the new chief fire officer, Clive Halliday, had arrived, got them all out of their machines, lined them up and was asking them questions. I said to him, 'Did you countermand my order of having the firemen sitting in their appliances?'

'Yes, I wanted to speak to them.'

'Wait till I tell you something, sir. If that bomb goes off now, we'll have maybe about twenty casualties. You fuck off back to Lisburn where you belong and don't come up here again until you learn something. I'm telling you, if that bomb went off, there could be half a dozen firemen killed with glass coming down on top of them from a five-storey building.'

So he went back to headquarters.

That afternoon Halliday was sitting with Raymond Moore, our ex-station commander. He says to Raymond, 'I was up in the city and they had a bomb scare and I did something wrong – the sub officer just nicely told me to fuck off back to Lisburn and stay there until I was sent for.'

And Raymond said to him, 'That must have been Jimmy Armstrong.' The next day Halliday drives into the yard, comes into the office and the first thing he did was shake my hand. He says, 'I never thought about what goes on. I've learnt more from that incident yesterday than I have in my entire career in the fire service.'

I says, 'You're welcome any time but don't countermand the orders of the officer on the ground in incidents like this here.'

Central Fire Station, Chichester Street, was beside the courts and the police station and was a large Victorian station. Damaged many time by bombs and struck by gunfire, it was, particularly at night, a world all its own, as Jimmy explains.

Chi backed on to Townhall Street and there was a back gate out of the station – the laundry gate. It opened out beside the back of Musgrave Street Police Station. The boys would go out through the gate to the pub around the corner, Roddy's, for a carry-out for the lads. It was John McCaughan, I think, went out this night for the beers. Anyway, about twenty minutes later, police, army, everything, arrived in the station yard saying that a bomb had been planted. So we started searching: searched the training school, searched the store, searching, searching everywhere … After a while Charlie Black says to the policeman, 'Who saw this bomb being planted?'

'A soldier,' he says, 'in the sanger, at the back gate there.'

And Charlie said, 'What did he see?'

'He seen a boy coming through with a big brown parcel.'

Charlie looks at him and said, 'Tell him to mind his own business in future. That was the carry-out.'

Some night's craic. A different world. It was only things like that which kept us sane.

Joe McKee

Joined the retained service in Carrickfergus in 1973 before moving to the whole-time service in Belfast one year later.

I did two years in the retained service in Carrick, mostly while I was a student. At the amalgamation of the old Northern Ireland Fire Authority and the Belfast Fire Brigade, I joined the whole-time service in Belfast, and I was posted to White Watch in Whitla Street, down at the docks. Belfast was a complete culture shock. The Belfast Fire Brigade was a very proud service. There were five stations in Belfast at that time, answerable to the former Belfast Corporation. The fire brigade was a department within the corporation, rather like the zoo or the gas service or the libraries. They were distinctive from other British and Irish fire brigades at that time in that all ranks, I think, wore white shirts. I remember in the time that I was there, in the new Northern Ireland Brigade, other ranks below station officer reverted to wearing blue shirts, and the old hands in the Belfast Fire Brigade were outraged. They were immensely proud of their long-held traditions, and I have to say that there was a looking-down on other stations outside Belfast. The only other full-time station was in Derry/Londonderry, and some of the Belfast men, I think, would admit that they regarded the rest of us as a bit like *Dad's Army*.

When I joined in '73, the Troubles had been going for just a few years. It was the time of the spectacular bombs that led to very large fires. My understanding was that, during the Troubles, the actual Troubles-related calls amounted to only about 10 per cent of all the mobilisations. But that 10 per cent of calls reflected almost 100 per cent of the really big fires and the big incidents. Though they weren't all big incidents – I remember in Carrickfergus, a bomb went off near a boarding house where working men stayed in inexpensive dormitory-type accommodation. They were up in an attic and the roof collapsed in on them. They ended up trapped in their beds by timber that came down on them.

I remember also going into a housing estate in Greenisland where a Catholic family were out at Saturday night Mass. The house was well alight, and the family dog, the pet, was found behind the front door. One of the fellas I worked with, who we would have regarded as a rough diamond, took the dog out on to the lawn at the front and he gave it mouth-to-mouth resuscitation. A hostile crowd formed round him and pointed out to him that it was a Catholic dog! With my sort of sheltered upbringing in County Antrim, I had never heard this sort of language before. These people genuinely believed that the dog, somehow, had a religious affiliation.

In Carrickfergus we were often sent up to Whitla Street Station to cover, when there were very large fires in Belfast, and all the fire engines in Belfast were tied up. That was the impact the Troubles had in this part of the world.

The very first incident that really shook me a bit was when I was in Whitla Street. There were often opportunities to go as a driver to Ardoyne Fire Station. Although there are a couple of fire stations covering West Belfast now, the old Ardoyne Station, behind Holy Cross Monastery and Church at the top of the Crumlin Road, used to cover Crumlin Road, Shankill Road – all of West Belfast – and it was a terrifically busy station. On 5 April 1975, the day of the Grand National, the Mountainview Tavern on the Shankill Road was blown up. We started work on the night shift at six o'clock. At twenty past six we were sent down to the pub. A bomb had gone off, the building had virtually collapsed and we had to recover five bodies. There was no fire, but we arrived at a scene of complete carnage. I remember another young firefighter, like myself, who was up from Omagh. We were confronted with a very elderly woman sitting on the street covered in little razor cuts due to the glass and we didn't know where to begin. We simply didn't know. We treated her sympathetically, as if she were our granny. How would we lift this woman? An ambulance crew came along, rolled out a sheet underneath her and scooped her up. She was alive, and they took her away, but that was my big first introduction to an incident involving several fatalities.

Paul McClelland

Was posted to White Watch at Central in Belfast at the start of his career, and spent all his service there.

To me, Central Fire Station in Chichester Street was the greatest station in the whole of the United Kingdom to serve in. It was renowned for being the most bombed fire station in all of Europe. We weren't actually the targets, we just had the misfortune of being right bang smack in the middle of the area with the high courts, the law courts, the police station and most of the Northern Ireland judiciary. We were just in the cross-hairs. That said, all the turnouts we had in central Belfast led to a level of expertise and a demonstration of courage and bravery way in excess of anything that would ever be repeated across the United Kingdom in the modern day. It was an honour to serve there and to serve alongside all those colleagues.

Station life itself was pretty routine. We were given a bit of a bye-ball regarding stringent work routines due to our workload. Stand-down time was split – people did their own thing. Some liked to watch videos, some liked to work on their cars, some did whatever they fancied. It just so happened that my clan liked to play poker all night but, as a consequence, we were always turning out within seconds, no matter what time of the night it was. Central Fire Station will always hold fantastic memories for those that served in it because of the extreme tomfoolery and pranks. Things that would never be repeated – they're gone forever. They would never be allowed to be repeated. On reflection, we were letting off steam because of the workload – because of what we were facing. Not only bombings, day in, week in, but also working under gunfire and in riotous situations. So Central has its place in history as far as I'm concerned, as do those who served in it.

I would say Central was the only civilian fire station in the United Kingdom that had bulletproof glass. A story comes to mind: a station officer had come over from England to attend an interview for a divisional officer posting. He was staying in what were lightly termed the training school buildings – temporary training school buildings in the old back part of Central. He'd come over that night, and he'd had his supper with us, and was curious about the bulletproof glass. Then he retired for the night and we completely forgot about him. Later that night we had to evacuate the station yet again because of a car bomb that had been parked between Central Station and the adjacent law courts. It had escaped everyone's mind that this man was still at the training school. Needless to say, once we'd evacuated and made our way round to our standby point for the appliances and personnel on the Laganbank Road, the bomb detonated. Bulletproof glass and bombs going off just didn't gel with the man – he decided to forgo the interview and headed back to England the next day.

Firefighting is very much a 'team sport'. We look after each other and trust that when things are tight, our mate will do whatever needs to be done to keep us safe – or save our life. Most incidents don't require such an acute level of teamwork, but every so often that's precisely what's needed.

One night Central got a call to Ideal Furnishings on the Lisburn Road as part of a make-up with Cadogan. We were responding to 'actuated 7/7s' – detonated bombs – and when we arrived, the premises were well alight. Numerous teams were committed to the upstairs, first-floor level, to fight the fire. Myself and Ray Farrell were one of the breathing apparatus teams, working in conjunction with at least two, possibly even four, other BA teams. As we moved through the building on the first floor with our jet, numerous incendiaries were continuing to explode so we had great difficulty penetrating the building and fighting the fire due to these explosions and the heat caused. It was a hard job. Nonetheless, given that we had the balls of a donkey, we pushed on.

Then it came to our attention that something had happened: we discovered that the leader of one of the other BA teams, Aidan, had fallen through some floorboards that had burnt away. They had given way under his weight. Luckily for Aidan, he was able to hang on to the hose that was across the hole and he was hanging on with his arms and legs wrapped round the jet like a monkey. So myself and Ray and the second member of Aidan's BA team attempted to get him back on to the floor but because we didn't know the extent of the burn underneath, we had to be very tentative in our approach. Low-pressure warning whistles started to sound on our BAs, which lent a great urgency to the situation. Given that we were deep inside a well-alight building with a colleague in dire need, we had to make a call. That call was to leave Aidan dangling! But with a purpose. Ray and the other BA team member stayed with Aidan, while I was tasked with making my way down to the appliances outside and informing them of the situation. I told them of the location and they immediately tasked another BA team, possibly two BA teams, to get inside the building and get underneath Aidan. They managed to locate him – they could see his back and ass as he dangled from the ceiling – and placed a bed below him. Aidan was then informed that they were going to drop him, hopefully, on to the bed. This building was previously a picture house so it had a very high ceiling. Aidan was told to let go. He did, luckily falling on to the bed with absolutely no injuries. He was retrieved and made it out of the building and, subsequently, it was the talk of the crews – the episode of the night. It was very nice that Aidan acknowledged the rescue. He presented myself and Ray with a handmade card – on which was a picture of three BA men looking down this hole with Aidan hanging on the branch – and two bottles of wine each. Personally, I thought he should have given us more – but it sufficed!

Like any organisation, the fire service is made up of many different types of people. Because we wear a uniform it's easy to assume that we are all similar in character. Of course, the reality is the complete opposite: there are the serious ones, the comedians and the sheer lunatics. It's that mix that makes the job so interesting …

A funny story comes to mind about Charlie Pye. Charlie was a character. We were having one of the busiest nights that I can ever remember in my time. At about six o'clock we were tasked – in fact nearly every fire engine in the whole of Belfast was tasked – to the Northumberland Street Mill. It had been torched and a massive fire had started. We were there maybe until twelve o'clock. Heading back to the station we got a cup of tea and we were immediately tasked to a persons reported – that's a different story. We were then tasked to another premises in Belfast, which although not well alight, was heavily smoke-logged. A small fire had occurred that had set off the sprinkler system and it had a very loud, clanging bell. Station Officer Douglas asked Charlie to 'knock the bell off'. As we were standing around we heard this massive clang and Charlie had knocked the bell clean off the wall with a sledgehammer, much to the consternation of wee Dougie.

Something similar occurred when we were at another persons reported in East Belfast. It was a reasonably bad house fire. Our pump crew was sent back to the station and the pump escape crew was hanging around while the officer in charge sorted out a few last bits and pieces and took the final details for his fire report. Charlie was asked to go and get the maul off the pump – the maul being another name for the sledgehammer. However, it was lost in translation. We were all sitting in the pump, keen to go back to the station, waiting for the driver, and Charlie, God love him, came and requested that we all go and see Station Officer Douglas. This caused some annoyance and a lot of expletives were directed towards Dougie. Charlie insisted that he wanted 'them all' off the pump. So we all headed in and Dougie wanted to know what *we* wanted!

It would be impossible now, many years later, to total up the number of bombs and incendiary attacks Belfast experienced during the Troubles, but it is likely to be in the thousands. Because of its location in the commercial heart of the city, Central Station probably attended a disproportionate number – not only incidents that occurred on its own patch, but to back up other stations at incidents in their respective areas. Its location beside the law courts and Musgrave Street Police Station also meant that it was routinely damaged during attacks on these other buildings. The station was severely damaged on a number of occasions and it was eventually isolated inside a section of closed-off street intended to protect the other buildings. Alas these security measures did not prevent further massive bombs from being left outside the front door.

One night we had to evacuate the station. Because of the way the appliances were parked at the station, the pump escape went first, followed by the emergency tender, followed by the turntable ladder, followed by the pump. This was maybe around the early hours of the morning, three o'clock, four o'clock in the morning, and the driver of the pump, remaining nameless, decided that he would stop at the red light on the traffic lights at the junction of Chichester Street and Oxford Street. This caused the other three appliances to back up, and have to sit and wait until the lights changed. I was on the pump and had the good fortune to be able to stare out the window at the car bomb ten feet away! I could hear numerous shouts of various expletives for the driver of the pump escape to ignore the fucking traffic lights and get out of the street. In due course we all arrived at the standby location, parked up, and were standing having a cigarette, chatting, when the bomb detonated. Some people ducked so hard they had to readjust their necks after they had disappeared down into their trunks. A hundred and fifty yards away from a massive explosion isn't far. And it was a huge explosion. From that time – if I remember it right – I think that it was agreed that the appliances would no longer be moved out of the station if it meant driving past a bomb, and that personnel would evacuate at the back via the police station.

There were numerous incidents we attended where the army bomb squad would have been deployed to make safe various bombs. Although they felt at times *we* were courageous, our courage was nothing compared to what these fellas were put through. The heavily-plated suits and headdresses were really only to keep their body intact because, if the bomb detonated at that range, it was fatal. I remember the ATOs brought in a new way of stopping the bomb going off by firing liquid nitrogen from the robot to freeze the device. On one such occasion on Donegall Square East, again in a building well alight, myself and my BA team were confronted by the ATO robot with said gun in place. We made a hasty retreat. The army ATO found it funny that they had discovered personnel inside this burning building: again, a significant degree of mutual respect!

It was very typical of Central, because of its location, that we heard bombs going off around Belfast city centre and we knew we were seconds away from being called. On one such occasion, in the early hours of the morning, we heard a bomb going off so we were prepared to head out. As expected, the turnout harmonics sounded, and the call was given as 'actuated 7/7s' in two locations at Cornmarket. Evans shop was one of them, but I can't recall the other one. It was a full attendance from Central – two pumps, emergency tender and turntable ladder. On that particular night I was on the emergency tender. The pump escape left the station, the TL left the station and the pump left the station – and we were sitting twiddling our thumbs, waiting and waiting for the officer in charge to arrive. We decided to wait no longer – there'd been a bit of a bollocks and he wasn't in the station. It was decided that I would take charge of the ET and head round to Cornmarket. In attendance at Cornmarket, bombs were continuing to actuate. One was at Brands & Normans shop, where it blew out on to the street just in front of Cadogan's crew, and another went off in Ann Street beside another crew.

At that particular incident our brand-new chief fire officer, Clive Halliday, who was from Wales, arrived down to 'meet the troops', as they say. Myself and Firefighter Tom Shaw were tucked into a doorway at Mooney's Bar – facing Evans, which was well alight – directing a jet at the fire. As I said, bombs had gone off while we were tucked in firefighting, and bombs had gone off further down Ann Street. As a result of the debris that had been scattered around the place our hose had developed a slight, reasonably noticeable burst, with water spraying out of the hole – but with no effect on the jet, it must be stressed. The chief, in his capacity as officer in charge, thought it was a good idea to ask if we had a hose bandage available? The height of the absolute nonsense of Clive's request for a hose bandage in that situation was matched by the reply, 'Clive, have you got a spare pair of knickers in your boot?' Clive promptly turned on his heel and walked off, somewhat confused.

Charlie McAuley
Joined the full-time service in 1978 and served in Belfast for the early part of his career.
At that time there were what we referred to in the fire service as 'auld hands', guys who had quite a bit of experience and had served a long time. They were maybe in their late forties or early fifties – old men to me as a young guy of twenty-two or twenty-three. They would have been there

to keep you right – to talk to you, to say to you, 'Look, these are the things that you will come across.' There was also a large number of young men who had come in with the intake in 1978–79 for the new watch. So quite a bit of lively camaraderie would have gone on; quite a bit of winding-up.

The old Chichester Street station was a big old station: the fire engines were on the ground floor; the middle floor was the galley area and our recreation area; and above were the dormitories. There were two sets of poles you slid down to get into the engine room – so there was quite a bit of horse play, much of which got missed by the command on the watch. Because it was such a big station, it was a wonderful building to work in – you could get up to a lot of silly things in it without anybody really knowing. That was part of the tension release. You had that comradeship. It built up the camaraderie with the watch because you knew the next fire call that you went to, you could be relying on the guy behind you to pull you out.

In the early years, when the fire-call came in, the alarm was sent to the station by harmonics – a beep-beep sound that came into the station over the speakers – and then there was an announcement made from the Lisburn Control Room. They would have announced the fire engine that was going and the type of call that it was going to, so you knew what you were attending and had a bit of a warning as to what you were likely to face. It could be anything: a suspect 7/7, actuated 7/7, building on fire, house on fire, persons reported, RTA, a child trapped in railings. One of the fire engines in Chichester Street was an emergency tender that carried all the specialist cutting equipment – all the automatic saws and heavy hydraulic equipment that you used for lifting or extracting things when people were involved in accidents. At that time you also had what you would call the run-of-the-mill calls – chimney fires, rubbish bins on fire – mixed in with the major fires. Once the harmonics went off on the station, once the call came in, there was that heightened sense of, right, we are going to something, and if you were told it was an 'actuated 7/7', you knew a bomb had gone off.

During my time in Belfast, I saw some major fires in the town and some bomb explosions. One in particular was up the Ormeau Road at the Errigle Inn on a Friday night. We had been turned out to a 'suspect 7/7' – it was believed there was a bomb. Usually you turned out and stood by while the army ammunition technical officer went in to deal with it. We were there for maybe two or three hours while the army dealt with the bomb – it was cleared and there was no fire. Exactly a week later, on that next Friday night, same thing again: 'suspect 7/7, Errigle Inn'. We were thinking we were going to be standing by there for another two hours, but this time we could see the smoke rising as we came up the Ormeau Road. The station officer said, 'Guys, we are getting a working fire here,' so as we pulled up we got to work. An aerial appliance was brought up as well and they set up in a side street to attack the fire. Myself and another firefighter, Jimmy Coleman, neither of us wearing breathing apparatus, were sent to take a jet in a side door and up a set of stairs. The fire was away at the rear of the building. So myself and Jimmy went up the stairs. We had a full jet beating this fire and doing a really good job holding the fire while the aerial appliance got into position to attack the fire from above – and the fire started to die down. Then the smoke started to clear and sitting in front of us was a bomb that we hadn't seen when we came in. You've never seen two guys move quicker – the jet was dropped and we took the stairs four at a time. When we got down we told the ATO that there was a bomb sitting at the top. We were fortunate – had that gone off, there would have been nothing left because we were in such a confined space.

Colin Taggart

Joined the full-time service in 1984. Although his service was relatively short – he left the brigade in 1989 to pursue academic study – he experienced the brutal reality of the Troubles close up. Two particular bombs have left him with vivid memories.

I was up at Knock on out-duty. We were watching *Neighbours* on the TV after lunch when the bomb went off. We heard it and started to move to the engine room, knowing it was likely to be something serious, but still strangely irritated that we were probably going to miss the end of the episode. We raced the short distance – blue light flashing, horns blaring – and arrived at this burning car with debris strewn around. A bomb had exploded under a retired police officer's car and he was partially thrown outside the vehicle. Somebody – I think it may have been a lollipop man who had been nearby – had already put a plastic mac over the man, assuming he was dead. It was clearly a bomb and there's sometimes a hesitation to approach things like that straightaway, but a fireman grabbed the hose and – right or wrong – we raced over and extinguished the fire, not thinking that there might have been another device or that the one that had gone off might only have been half-exploded.

We were close in to the car when somebody shouted out, 'I think he moved.' Immediately we took the mac off him and a vision and stench of hell greeted us. An auld hand said, 'It's only nerves, mucker, he's probably just sliding off the seat.' He was still alive, barely, but it was all too obvious he couldn't survive it. It remains one of the most distressing things I experienced – to be close in beside this man, knowing that no matter what we or the ambulance crew did, he could only live for a few more minutes.

Nevin Donaghy and I were on our way to Central Station one afternoon to go on duty at six o'clock – we always came into Belfast from the Holywood side and cut over the Queen's Bridge – but, as we were approaching the bridge in the slow, rush-hour traffic, a bomb exploded just to our right on Middlepath Street. We pulled up, got out and ran over. It was obvious straightaway that it was an under-car booby-trap bomb that had just detonated, and the car was on fire with the driver inside. We were in our uniform for parade not our firefighting kit, but it must have been pretty obvious that we were firemen anyway – but there was absolutely nothing we could do. It was hopeless. The bomb was only about three hundred yards from Central and almost immediately we could hear the pumps' sirens as they turned out to the call. We stayed until they arrived and then got back into Nevin's car and went to the station. Normally when we get to a scene like that we're ready and able to actually do *something* – maybe even save a life – so it was a strange experience to be as helpless as everybody else that was there and also to feel a particular pressure because we were in uniform. It turned out later that I knew the victim – he had given me career advice prior to joining the brigade.

The fire service is the sort of job that either appeals or doesn't and during the Troubles that was probably even more acutely the case: you loved it or you shouldn't be in it. The younger you were when you joined, the stronger that attitude became and the more the camaraderie and moments of high drama drew you in. For Colin, it certainly had that effect.

Looking back, there was a mixture of terror, excitement, boredom and glamour. It wasn't all about rescuing half-naked damsels in distress from the top of burning buildings; nor is it true that all the nice girls love a man in uniform, but we certainly tested the theory. We regularly conducted safety inspections and hydrant tests in the city; sometimes at Queen's University. Being a part-time student there, it did no harm to my reputation to be seen as a member of the team who regularly featured on the nightly news keeping Belfast safe during a very dangerous time.

In between fire calls and drills there was always the opportunity for mischief too. The old Victorian structure of

Central, with its narrow alleys and drill tower, lent itself to one of the great distractions of the watch: water bombing. This required skill, courage and deceit as the victim – whether the intended target or not, and especially if it was an officer – did not usually see the funny side. A large balloon filled with water dropped from thirty metres up would not only drench everything and everybody in the area but was also startling and infuriating. It could happen at any time of the day or night – there were many smiling assassins and the quick escape provided by the poles meant the suspect was hard to identify. When working together for long periods in difficult situations, your colleagues can drive you nuts, but I only realised the value of those bonds of common cause after I left.

On my last day as I cleared out my locker, everybody was on parade at the back of the engine room in Central Fire Station. They all saw me leave, but as they were standing in line to attention they couldn't gesture as I walked out the back gate for the last time. The hairs on the back of my neck stood up as it really sunk in that I was leaving, and that I'd never again be part of that 'band of brothers'. That always sticks in my mind.

Heather Smart

Joined the full-time service in 1991, becoming Northern Ireland's first female firefighter. She spent all her service at Red Watch, Knock Fire Station in East Belfast.

I had worked in the Royal Victoria Hospital as a physiological measurement technician in cardiology for just over three years but I wasn't getting what I needed out of the job, so I looked about to see where else I could work. I had taken part in the fire prevention quiz that was held nationwide when I was in third form in school. We had won the heat in Northern Ireland and then we had won the Northern heat in Glasgow, and then we went down to London and actually won the whole thing. So that gave me a very positive first view of the fire brigade. The officer who trained us, leading fireman Harry Martin, was responsible for getting us all together and making sure we studied what we were supposed to. He was a great help and when I joined the fire brigade I had that positive memory of working with the service.

When I joined, it was just a matter of keeping my head down and getting on with the work. I had to prove to myself that I could do the job – but I also had to prove to everybody else that I could do it. All I wanted to do was keep my head below the parapet and get on with it, but of course that wasn't quite what happened, and I always felt that there were people watching to see how I was getting on. Some people were keen to see me do well, but I think perhaps there were others who just had a different idea of what the fire brigade was about and couldn't see that there was a place for women in the job. It was a mixed picture – there were one or two guys on the watch who made life a bit difficult but there were more who wanted to help me, like my station officer, Arthur Plumpton, and Jackie Smith, one of the 'auld hands', who always treated me fairly.

I started in 1991, so I was working in the job during the Drumcree unrest. I remember an incident in East Belfast when a car showroom was on fire. When we turned up, both the army and the police were in attendance on the street corners. We worked hard. There were maybe three or four fire engines there and we worked hard to put all the cars out. In the midst of all that, there was a sudden flurry of movement and the police and the army withdrew. Nobody told us that this was because there had been a shot fired – so we were left standing with our hoses wondering what was going to happen next!

There were periods of time when the placing of incendiaries in shops was near enough routine. One particular night, when quite a few of the shops in the centre of Belfast had been hit, we were just going from call to call.

We went to a commercial premises at the bottom of Peter's Hill to back up another crew who were there ahead of us and had got to work by the time we arrived. It was at least a four-storey building with a big, wide, fancy staircase. In order to get to the fire we had to fight our way through water that was flowing down the stairs – one of the crews had been squirting water at what they believed was the fire, but they'd been hitting some big mirrors instead. It was a busy night and everyone was tired and there was a lot going on – anything could happen. On a night like that you'd be constantly mobilised to different calls and there wouldn't be time to go back to the station for toilet breaks or food or anything else – you would just literally be turned out call to call. Controls would ask if there were any free appliances and if you were able to go or within a few minutes of being able to go, you would let them know and they would send you on to the next fire call. So there were times that we wouldn't get back to the station at all.

Firefighters at the scene of the bomb attack and fire at the La Mon Ho Hotel, February 1978. *(PA Images)*

THE EAST

Bangor

Although relatively affluent and in a desirable location well away from the street violence and near anarchy of Belfast, Bangor still suffered considerably during the Troubles. Its shops and businesses were 'commercial targets' for bombs and incendiaries, and there were direct attacks on members of the security forces. Even in this otherwise peaceful town, the Troubles left their mark.

Derrick Murray

Joined the retained service in Bangor in 1952 and retired in 1986.
The first big incidents we had were the fire bombs in Wellworths and the Co-operative. It was really tough going for a while. I remember George Morrison, the chief, saying that at one time there were twenty-six jets out at those incidents – and that's a big fire. There was a lot of damage done then. A couple of the firemen came out of Wellworths and they were so exhausted, they lay down. A policeman and policewoman came along and talked to them for a while. Then they disappeared – they went along Queen's Parade to a chip shop and brought them back fish suppers in the police car.

The big bombs were hard to deal with. The police got the report of a car bomb in Main Street, and Tom, a friend of mine who was in charge of the police at the time, was out searching cars. Brave man – he got into one of the suspect cars at the bottom of Main Street and discovered that the bomb was in the backseat so he made a hasty retreat. It went off shortly after. I was on the second appliance and we were told definitely not to go down Main Street. The first appliance had gone down Main Street past the second car bomb – we didn't know that at the time – and we were told to go Hamilton Road, Prospect Road, High Street and Quay Street to get to the bottom of Main Street. It could easily have been a real disaster. Actually, when the second bomb went off at a distance of maybe three hundred yards from the station, a part of the car landed in the fire station yard. Part of the chassis was buried in the side of a shop opposite – buried right in, right through into the brick work. It was a nasty time; they were hairy situations, they really were. But, thankfully, there were no serious injuries.

There were three car bombs in the town and the third one was opposite Menarys in Main Street, just opposite the GPO. I'd recently been injured in a fire and I was on crutches. I'd actually walked past the car. I got down Market Street and the police came down the street with loud hailers. 'Clear the streets! Clear the streets!' I made my way round to the fire station – I wasn't able to go on the appliance of course – but I did duty officer and took all the calls etc. A young fireman from Donaghadee came in the station. He said, 'I'm from Donaghadee station – could I help?' I said, 'See that locker over there, that's my locker. Get my gear on and away you go'.

When the third one went off it lifted the roof of the GPO up and down again. And they got part of the engine of the car that blew up at Wardens' Corner, which is a distance of maybe three hundred yards. Things might have been different – I might not have been here to tell the story had the bomb gone off as I passed the car.

We got a call to Donaghadee one day. There used to be a garage on the left-hand side going into the town. It was a two-tiered garage: there was a shop, then down the stairs was the actual garage where the work was going on, just on the shore side. A bomb had gone off in it. We arrived down and we went into the garage below to set up a searchlight. We were taking cars out, when the station officer puts his head over the rail and shouts, 'Boys, we've just got word there's another bomb to go off.' Well, I stopped running about halfway down the Warren Road. In a case like that, you don't stand on ceremony, you get out! Fortunately enough there'd just been the one bomb – but we didn't know that at the time.

Things were strange in those days. We had a chimney fire in a bungalow that had a bay window. The boys had put the ladder up and they were going to run up the roof ladder but I said, 'Look, you don't need the roof ladder. Walk the ladder back a bit, up on to the roof of the bay window and you're at the chimney.' We were walking the ladder back and I happened to look up, and the top extension of the ladder broke loose and got me in the chest. Put me out cold. They rushed me to the hospital in one of the boy's cars. It was Sammy McCullough who took me up. There was a UDA roadblock near the Ulster Hospital so Sammy stopped at it. The boys came over to the van, masks on. Sammy told them, 'There's an injured fireman here. We're taking him to the hospital'. And this boy, I couldn't say who he was – I wasn't paying much attention to who it was – stuck his head in through the window and he said, 'Awk, hello Derrick. How are ya?' I didn't know to this day who he was, but he knew me and 'away you go,' he said.

Because I had some first aid training, I joined the Red Cross and I used to drive their ambulance. At the weekends it was usually made available at the hospital. I would check into the hospital on a Saturday night and answer whatever calls came through. One time, I'd just collected the ambulance and my nurse and pulled into Bangor Hospital. I went to sit down when the switchboard said to me, 'Don't bother sitting down – there's a call coming through.' A woman had been injured by a bomb on High Street. All the streets were closed off at the security gates at the time, but the police had all the gates open for us. Turned out that the victim was a policewoman – she'd been walking up High Street with a policeman. She'd been on the inside. The cylinder bomb was on the windowsill of Fealty's Bar. It went off and she got part of the cylinder in her chest. Twenty-six years of age. Lovely looking girl she was. She was badly injured and had lost a lot of blood. We rushed her to the hospital, but we knew she was gone. My wife, Jean, when I came home, said she'd never seen me as angry. A young life taken. It was the same in so many cases where bombs went off. Here's a young person, helping her country, you know, blown out of existence – for what?

Sometimes in the middle of all the terrible stuff, you got a laugh. We got a call this night and I was in the second appliance, standing by. It was Holywood's call. I said to the duty man, 'Where's the call?' and he replied, 'Bomb in the Culloden Hotel.' I rang up headquarters and told them, 'I look after this place, the maintenance. I'll head up. I'll be more good there than sitting here'. Headquarters give me the okay to go ahead so I got into the car and away I went. When I arrived up at the Culloden the road was all closed off, but the police let me through. When I pulled up, Chief Fire Officer George Morrison was at the gates going into the hotel. I reported to him. He said, 'Good, Derrick. Get your gear on. The ATO is on his way and you'll be able to help him'. I spoke to a few of the staff who told me where the bomb was. The ATO arrived and the chief introduced me to him: 'This is Fireman Murray. He knows the hotel. He does work in it – he'll take you in and show you where the bomb is'. I was nearly going to get back into the car and go home again! But the ATO said, 'No, just tell me where it is'. Then he asked if he could drag the bomb out and I said no. He asked why and I said, 'There's a flight of stairs up to the room. There's two steps up into the room. The bomb is in the bottom of the wardrobe, which is six inches off the ground.' He asked me a few other questions and I was able to tell him.

We all had to go outside then, hide behind the appliances, and the word came through, 'Right, I am coming out.' He came out carrying this thing, took it off down to the bottom of the garden and set it off. Then Mr Billy Hastings, the owner, arrived on the scene and he was really most appreciative of what had been done. I didn't think he would recognise me with my firefighting gear on, but he did – he came straight over. Now the manager was Mr Weston and Mr Hastings asked, 'Derrick, has Mr Weston made provision for the boys to have a drink?'

And I said, 'Well, he brought drink in.' In those days there was a room as you go into the Culloden on the left, a private lounge. I said, 'He set up tables in there'.

Mr Hastings replied, 'That's no good – open the bar in there, the main bar.'

Everybody was ushered in. I can't even remember who all was there, but the Holywood Brigade were there, we were there, the army were there, the ATO – different appliances. That night Mr Hastings showed his appreciation to all concerned in a very generous way.

Sammy McCullough

Joined the retained service in Bangor in 1968.

I used to be in the motor trade, served my time as a motor mechanic, then served in the parts service. I was in the fire service from '68 but it was only twelve hour then – six at night until six in the morning. Then the sub officer, Joey Thompson, who was a cobbler in Central Avenue, asked me could I go twenty-four hour as I lived very near the station. I asked my boss if he could see a way to let me get out for fires. He couldn't see his way to letting me go. At that time the council had been advertising for staff for the new swimming pool. I had a fair bit of experience with the swimming club, so I applied and I got the job as a recreation attendant. I was only there a month and a half and I became the foreman, then not long after that I became the supervisor. Once I was with the council, I was transferred on to twenty-four-hour availability for fire calls. I had two foremen under me – they knew that every so often I disappeared, and they covered for me when I was away to a fire. The pool was really close to the fire station. I worked like that for years and we had quite a number of serious fires.

One night one of the pumps was sent to Newtownards and we got a call to bring the other pump down to a chippy on Queen's Parade. We got the hydrant set into the pump because we knew it was going to be a good one – I remember going up to the door and bringing up the foam branch and the next thing, who was beside me but George Morrison, the chief. And he says to me, 'Don't go near that – look at the glass on those doors.' The glass on the doors was all swollen out. George warned me that they were going to blow; that there was going to be a big fire flash, and he was right – my enthusiasm could have been costly.

One time they did the town with incendiary bombs. They knew they were going to get caught, so they went into Barry's Amusements and dumped them behind all the machines, all the one-armed bandits. The lady who owned it was going about, panicking like mad. We were sent in with the long-handled litter pickers, picking out the incendiaries and setting them into buckets, carrying them out to a concrete bollard. The ATO was lifting them out and snipping the wire with his pliers. Buckets of them we carried out. They could have gone off in our hands – we could have been roasted.

At another call in Bangor – at the Bel One, where the new garden centre is now – they'd been in and left these incendiaries and most of the furniture was quite damaged. We had the jets in, got it all out, cleared up, thinking nothing of it. We're all made up ready to go when all of a sudden I happened to look in and see smoke going in the corner. And do you know what they had done? They had actually pulled out those big rolls of carpet, put the incendiaries behind them, and then rolled them back in. These had all started igniting and we couldn't get the fires out because they were coming out of the ends of the carpets. What we had to do was put breathing apparatus on again and go in and pull the carpets off the racks until we knew where the fires were and use the hose reels to put them out. Better that than driving back to the station and getting called out again – embarrassing enough that we'd missed it.

I remember the big fire at Barry's Amusements in Bangor. We were on the second pump. We'd arrived at Crosby Street and run the lines down and got the jets going. There were three of us on jets and the sub officer, he was in front of us. I was pulling the hose down the outside lane, and I think there were two guys still in there behind this gable. I looked up and saw this big crack appearing in the top window and I remember screaming, 'Run!' The two guys looked round at me and dropped their hoses and they ran for me but Eric wasn't quick enough. The gable wall came down. It fractured his ankle. He didn't get out in time, but I was straight in there, pulled all the rubble off him till we got him out and then took him round the front to the ambulance. He was seconds away from being killed.

In the retained we used to have annual inspections. We used to work for about three weeks ahead of it – unders were painted, mudguards were painted, wheels were painted, ladders were taken off and shining, locker doors like mirrors. Everything had to be spick and span. When George Morrison was chief, he used to come at night from about three weeks ahead to see how we were getting on. I was the leading fireman and I was in charge of the Land Rover crew, and we had her shining. But when Morrison had completed the inspection, he said, 'I'm afraid that I've found a serious fault with the Land Rover.' I nearly died. 'No fault to the crew or anyone involved,' he said, 'but in below one of the battery terminals I found a wee spot of green corrosion.' You know, right in behind the battery. And he'd watched us for three weeks to see if we'd spot it and catch on. So we'd failed. I was absolutely mortified. He certainly ran a tight ship. That was him showing that he was paying attention.

Sammy retired in 1989 as the result of a serious injury sustained while he was on duty.

I had a big fall on 30 November 1987. I was badly hurt at the Queen's Court Hotel in Bangor – I fell off the back roof. I fell forty feet and sustained a lot of serious injuries. It was about half past three in the morning. Sub Officer John Cherry and I were on the roof at the back of the old Bangor Engineers' Club, surveying the situation – we knew we were in big trouble because the flames were about thirty foot above us. We had to get up ladders to get on to the roof because the access was very limited. John and I were planning to get the hydraulic platform down from Belfast because the flames were so high. We were discussing this when John turned to face me. I stepped to the side and fell down a light shaft, past all these windows, and landed on a lean-to roof. That saved my life. I landed on about three inches of pigeon dirt – that was my cushion – but even with that I finished off being very badly hurt. My right hand was smashed, pretty much severed and I had broken ribs and a broken pelvis. My helmet didn't come off and that saved my face.

We'd no access in or out so the guys had to rope me on to a ladder to get me out – carried me across the roofs and down the ladder and into the ambulance. I knew both the paramedic, Margaret, and the driver, Walter, because I was about thirty years in the Red Cross. I didn't find this out until a year later, but one of the guys said that my heart had stopped once as we were going up the Bryansburn Road on the way to the hospital and another time just outside the Ulster Hospital – Margaret brought me back. Thanks to her I am alive. To repair my hand, the surgeon, Mr McAfee took bones and nerves from my leg to make my hand work again. He was able to put me back together again. A lovely man. He told me that if it hadn't been for the experience he'd had during the worst of the Troubles, I might not have made it.

Castlereagh

On the eastern outskirts of Belfast, Castlereagh Fire Station was a bit of an anomaly. Until 1973, Belfast had two fire services. Belfast City Council funded and operated the Belfast Fire Brigade that provided the service within the municipal boundary, while the Fire Authority for Northern Ireland ran the service everywhere else. Because the Castlereagh area was outside the city limit (even though it was regarded by most locals as being a suburb of Belfast), the Fire Authority had to provide a service to its residents. Castlereagh Fire Station was built for that specific purpose and staffed as a retained station. Probably most of the serious incidents its crews attended were actually in the city, but one that was closer by remains among the very worst of the Troubles.

Teddy Colligan
Spent twenty-seven years in the retained service in Castlereagh.
We moved into our new house about 1958 and I often saw my new next-door neighbour charging out when the fire station siren went. I got to know him, and he thought it would be a good idea if I joined Castlereagh Fire Station – a two-pump retained station on Ladas Drive. It was quite a drive down from where I lived, but I had no problem making the time that I needed to reach the station. So I put in an application and in no time at all I was a retained fireman. I was in Castlereagh until I left in 1988. I worked in ICL, a computer firm on Montgomery Road, and they provided eighteen people from the factory – eighteen people were all coming from the one factory and staffing Castlereagh Fire Station. When the factory closed, we scattered about a bit, but we were still able to respond to the station. We responded at that time to a siren, and then years later we got the little bleepers, which made such a difference to turning out.

Before the Troubles it was quiet. You got chimney fires, you got gorse fires, you got maybe fires on a farm and things like that, along with chip pan fires, kitchen fires and the like – just the normal run-of-the-mill calls, like any other town. You might have got one or two calls in a week, maybe some weeks you got one call, some weeks you maybe got six or seven calls. There was no pattern to it at all. Things changed dramatically when the Troubles started. Being on the outskirts, just on the edge of Belfast, we might as well have been a Belfast station because we were in Belfast as much as we were in our own area. It started for us with a lot of car fires, and a lot of cars being burnt and used as barricades.

One of the earliest bombs we got was at the big substation on the top of the hill above Castlereagh. As far as I remember it was during a loyalist strike or something ... I think it was a loyalist attack on the transformer, probably to switch the lights off in the area. We walked into it that day! We came up the Castlereagh Road and we could see the smoke but weren't sure where it was. We didn't get a lot of information – we thought at worst it was a farm – and when we got up to the transformers ... There's something like seventy thousand, eighty thousand gallons of cooling oil goes through the transformers to keep them cool – and that's what was on fire! It was an absolutely amazing experience. We went in but we didn't really know what we were doing or what we were dealing with.

We got spanners and started to take the inspection covers off. It was just a massive flame inside. We were using foam. There were big massive steel tanks, and it was like walking on the deck of a ship. Big screws and plates and covers all over, and it was so hot that we walked right through the soles of our boots and had to get new ones sent from Lisburn. What we didn't realise either was that the water out of the ruptured tanks was running into our water supply – so we were taking water from a river that was being flooded by thousands and thousands of gallons of oil. At one stage we were wondering why we were losing foam. We couldn't make the foam. Then we discovered that we were bringing up the oily water to try and make foam, which didn't work. But that was a big fire. That was an amazing fire.

We sometimes came under attack. We had armed men in the machine. We had equipment stolen out of the machine, and we nearly lost the machine at one stage when we were trying to deal with a fire at the Bass Charrington brewery. We tried to get to the fire but there were burning barricades at the top of Kennedy Way and we couldn't get through. We turned round and gave a radio message back to headquarters that we couldn't reach the fire. We had a code for that. As we turned and drove away, we were followed down Kennedy Way by a wee Volkswagen that pulled over in front of us and braked hard. Some boys jumped out and said, 'Where do you think yous are going?'

'Well, we're going back to the station. We can't get in.'

'We'll get you in, c'mon' – and they jumped in and sat on top of the engine covers and they were all armed, and they took us back up to the fire and we dealt with it.

The camaraderie with the boys and all was great – it was first class. I mean, you might have only seen them for two hours training on the Monday night, and then you could have had a week when you didn't have a call until the following Monday night. But then we got a tremendous number of calls during the Troubles. As retained firefighters in this station on the outskirts of Belfast, we actually turned out to more calls than some of the full-time guys in the Belfast stations. I chummed about all my adult life with a guy who was in our station originally, and then worked in Central Fire Station. We used to compare notes and I had more calls during the week than he had because he was on for a shift, while I was on for twenty-four hours. So I was getting calls twenty-four hours a day, whereas he was only getting calls during his watch.

I'll give you one funny story. We were turned out to Central Fire Station one dinnertime to back them up, and we arrived at the station with two pumps from Castlereagh. We reversed the appliances into the station, then went upstairs to the billiard room for a game of billiards. The meals for the crews who had been sent to a call were all laid out and the girl in the kitchen said, 'You needn't let those dinners go to waste, boys – get stuck in!' We all lifted a plate off the counter and got stuck in. We were halfway through the meal when we heard the doors downstairs opening. It was a false alarm the boys had gone to – and we'd just eaten their dinner! I think it was beans on toast for the crews that night. You did have some funny experiences; it wasn't all doom and gloom.

On 17 February 1978, the IRA left bombs attached to cans filled with petrol on the windowsills of a function room at the La Mon House Hotel.

At this stage, going to big fires in Belfast would have been frequent – often commercial property and hotels, and then hotels in our own area as well. We had quite a few hotels in our area that were burnt. We had lost a few even before La Mon, but the incident there was probably the most devastating, for us, as firemen. La Mon had started out as a small family business, run by a girl that I actually worked with in the factory. We used to go there and have a meal in it, and I had been at a dinner dance there the week before. It would have been our local place to go for a night out. It's only a mile up the road from where we live.

When we got to it the place was well alight, very well alight. There was always a water problem in the area around La Mon. There was always a pressure problem. We knew there was no way we were going to get enough water out of the hydrants, so we used an 'LPP' – a light portable pump – in the river. Just as you go into La Mon there is a little river that runs underneath the driveway and we had the pumps in there for the whole night. From what we were told, the fire started with cans of petrol and explosives on the cans of petrol. The windows at the front of the hotel ran right down almost to the floor and the bombs were apparently just set on the windowsills. There was a long function room and it was burning from end to end. We had no chance of saving anyone in it at that time. No way you were getting into the building. The building was well alight: too well alight for anyone to get in … to even attempt to do a rescue. It was so … so devastating … so fierce. It was really a very fierce fire. We got a bit of a break later in the night and then we were back the next day to clear up. In broad daylight it wasn't … it wasn't a nice scene. It does stick in your mind a bit, so it does. Probably out of all of the incidents that we had, that was probably the worst one that we experienced. Twelve people died.

Many deaths during the Troubles have long disappeared from the collective consciousness of even local Northern Ireland people. All these deaths were tragic, but some were perhaps all the more sorrowful for the fact that simple good intentions, like wanting to save possessions, could cost so dearly. Mary Thompson's death on 6 December 1971 was one such tragedy.

There was no counselling, there was nobody giving you any advice about anything. Despite this, to my knowledge I don't think any of the boys had any effects from any of the experiences – nobody has ever spoken to me about it. I never had any myself, never. It never affected me at all. One or two things stick in the mind, though, one or two things, but for me it's not La Mon, it's not the big fire at the transformer: it's another incident in the centre of Belfast when a gable wall came down on top of people that I had been speaking to five or ten minutes before, and we had to dig them out with our hands. We had a building on the Dublin Road that was on fire after a bomb had gone off and it was beside the Salvation Army citadel. I was a leading fireman and I was in charge of a crew. One of my crew members asked me to come up on to an adjoining roof where he was working. He thought that the gable end of the next building was swaying about. It could also have been the fact that the smoke going past it giving that effect. I knew that people were trying to save band instruments down in the Salvation Army so I ran down and I advised them to get out, but before they came out, the building came down on top of them and a woman died. So that's probably the worst incident, the worst incident that I – well, it still sticks in my mind, the fact that they didn't come out when I asked them to. That's probably the worst one for me: you're digging out people that you were talking to a short time before from under a massive big pile of bricks. Afterwards, there was a lot of confusion about who said what to who – but that doesn't make it any easier for me.

There were times when you came back to the station and it was very quiet. Particularly after the likes of Le Mon, Dublin Road or explosions. It's something we never talked about, how you felt after an incident. You know it's just … I mean we've had cars blow up with people in them and we've gathered up the remains and things like that. It wouldn't have been the same sort of shouting and bantering that you would have got if you had been up at a chimney fire or something like that. That's probably the only effect that you would really have seen in the boys: that everybody was very quiet – you got your gear off and went home. I always thought, 'You put the uniform on and you change completely.' You're there to do a job, and that's it. You just went on with … you just went on with your life. You just went on with things.

Frank Lowry
Joined the retained service in Castlereagh in 1962 and retired in 1988.
Jackie Simpson, who worked with us at ICL, had joined the service. My wife and I had just married and moved into Orangefield, and Jackie said to me, 'Why don't you join

the fire brigade? You get such-and-such amount, pays your rates,' and they were looking for men at the time. But, over the years, I've realised that I would have done it for nothing. It was just so good. You got a good feeling when you went to a person's house and even if it was only a chimney fire, you know, you could see how glad they were to see you – maybe even crying with relief when we turned up. I joined in 1962 and retired in 1988. I would have done it for nothing – it was great. I can't thank Jackie enough for that – he went to Australia and we're still in contact with him. As I said, I would have done it for nothing, although my daughter and my wife ... see the nights that I was out, maybe all night, they couldn't sleep, especially when there were bombs going off all over the place. They didn't know what was happening. It was hard for them.

We were called out one night to the bottom of the Ravenhill Road, to the big pub there, just opposite the Short Strand. The fire was going really well and we were doing our best to put it out and the next thing we heard bullets flying down. Jack Smith, one of our senior officers, came down and said, 'Right, boys, just leave it. Back to the station.' They wouldn't let us stay. There was another one on the Ormeau Road, a cake shop that got attacked. I had the ladder up to the window at the front and I remember the officer saying, 'Get the hell down, the whole thing's going to explode.' And again he wouldn't let us go any further. The chief at the time was George Morrison. He turned up to quite a few fires with us and one thing about him: he knew everybody's name. He'd have come in and he maybe wouldn't have seen us for a couple of months and it was, 'Hello Frank,' 'Hello Roy' – it was amazing. I thought, 'How the hell does he do that?' I thought he was brilliant.

There was a large bomb set off in a shirt factory on the Dublin Road and it started a huge fire – probably one of the largest in the city since the Blitz. I can't remember whether we were sent as part of the make-up or as a relief crew, but when we were there, I went into the building beside the factory – the Salvation Army building – with Roy Simpson, who was the sub officer in Castlereagh at the time. There was a lady moving furniture about. She was trying to get chairs and band instruments out. She was an older woman, and we were talking to her and saying, 'We'll have to get you out,' and she said, 'Yes, okay, I'm coming now,' and then a fire officer came in and said to me and Roy, 'Right, boys, out. This wall's not secure – it's going to come down.' We were just walking up the aisle and all of a sudden the whole thing collapsed and that wee woman had no chance of getting out. Roy and I were actually with her moments before the thing came down. She had no chance – it was just a mess – she'd taken the full load of the wall on her. She died and we had a very narrow escape.

I drove the first appliance to La Mon. We got it just as a bomb explosion. But we did know … we were told that there were people inside. First of all we couldn't get water – we had to search out on the main road for a hydrant and then we had to get it to a pump and then by the time we did … all we had was the water in the appliance. Obviously that ran out in no time. We ended up getting water from the river. When we got inside, it was horrible because I honestly didn't see any bodies – everything was so bad. We knew there were bodies. It was horrific. Whenever we really got into it, it was, I would say, four or five in the morning, coming up to daylight. You couldn't make out anything inside. I honestly cannot remember any fireman taking bodies out – and as I said, we were the first. I think they may have been left *in situ* for police to do their forensic stuff.

La Mon was awful, but probably the main Troubles event that has stuck in my mind is a fire at Corry's, the timber yard, on the Springfield Road. Not for the first time, we were in Chichester Street Fire Station, standing by, and I think it was quite late at night. Again, I was driving and we got the call. It was to a bungalow on fire at the back of Corry's yard. As soon as we drove into the street there were guys with rifles and they stopped us and said, 'Right, at the top of the street there's a bungalow on the left-hand side that's on fire. You can put your water on that but no water on the yard. We'll let you put the fire out in the bungalow.' That was a bit unusual, but okay, and we got the water on. About ten or fifteen minutes later all I see is a fire engine flying down the street. It was our fire engine – somebody had jumped in, drove it down the street and stopped, and we didn't know at the time but they'd got on to control. Anyway, the boys with the guns told us to stand there. They told us not to put any more water on the bungalow. Then a priest come down. He said, 'Who's driving?' and I said, 'I am,' and he asked my name and I told him, Frank. He said, 'Just hang on.' He went away for about fifteen or twenty minutes and when he came back, he said, 'Francis, you get in, and if I say go, just go and don't stop – straight out.' Fair enough – we did just that. We didn't know until we got back to the station that they'd said they were going to shoot us. We knew that we weren't allowed to put water into Corry's, but later we heard they'd said that if they didn't withdraw the brigade, they were going to shoot us. But we all got out and we got all the kit out with us. Funny thing about that too, not long after, I was getting the *Reader's Digest* and there was an article in it about the fire at Corry's and the fire brigade and all that happened. Didn't expect that.

During the strike in 1977, Ray Priestley, one of the union reps from Central, came up to Castlereagh and he said what was going on, and that they didn't want us to turn out, because in Belfast the full-time ones weren't turning out, so the officers in controls were obviously going to send for us. I think probably about three of us said okay and didn't turn out, realising if they got the money they were going for, we'd obviously get a rise too. But the rest of them did turn out and after that, every time Castlereagh went into any of the other stations to stand by or whatever, they were ignored. I couldn't blame them. They knew that I had supported them so it didn't affect me really, but the rest of the crew had to take it. Roy Simpson, the sub officer, was a good friend of mine, but the number of rows we had over that was unbelievable. He thought he was doing the right thing and so did I.

You hear about firemen taking time off after a particular experience. We were never like that. We saw some terrible things and I can't remember any of the firemen in Castlereagh ever doing that. Even after La Mon. And if the siren had gone half an hour later – we'd have been away again. Even today when I think back and remember all the things, I'm all right. It was my job and I had to do it and some things were horrible, but I don't think it has really affected me in any way. I cannot remember any person in Castlereagh Station who couldn't do the job after being at a bad incident. The next day they would have been just the same: if the siren lifted they were out again.

Epilogue
John Wilson

I worked in the fire service for thirty years, and there is one particular night from early in my career that has always stayed with me.

One evening in the early eighties, just after we had started our night shift, there was a loud bang. A car bomb had exploded in a street near the city hall and within minutes we were tackling a large fire. The adrenalin pumps at times like this, and when you're young and keen you can't get enough of it. I loved every moment. At one point we had to evacuate the building and as we waited for the all-clear, we stood around and chatted. I overheard someone saying, 'That was bad earlier today, wasn't it?' Not having a clue what he was talking about, I asked what had happened and it turned out that a young person had been killed in an explosion outside Belfast. I felt sick. There was me thinking that this mayhem was good crack – one big thrill-ride – and somewhere else a poor family's heart had been ripped out.

The simple truth is that for every incident we go to and get a real buzz from, there's a victim. Firefighters are just normal people and in the excitement of the moment and all the camaraderie, it's easy to overlook that reality. The comfort I take from my own experiences and from conversations over the years with colleagues is that we somehow manage not to lose sight of this. As these stories close, it's right to acknowledge that, while we thrive on the excitement, we know we are here first and foremost to help people – and we also know what a privilege that is.

Biographical notes

JIMMY ARMSTRONG joined the full-time service in Belfast in 1965. Most of his service was operational with some periods spent in fire safety. The largest part of his service was spent in Central Fire Station and he retired at the rank of sub officer in 1996. Jimmy and his wife Mary live in the Rusheyhill area of Dundrod and he continues to enjoy golf, fishing and the GAA.

ALAN BROWN joined the retained service in Newtownards in 1957. In 1962 he joined the full-time service and was based in Central Fire Station until his retirement in 1987. He received a Chief Fire Officer's Commendation for his rescue of two colleagues from the roof of the Co-op building in Belfast following a bomb attack and fire in May 1972. Alan lives in Newtownards and enjoys restoring old cars and light commercial vehicles.

PETER CLARKE joined the volunteers fire station in Crossmaglen in 1972. The station was assimilated into the Northern Ireland Fire Brigade's retained service in 1979. He retired in 1984. Peter's full-time occupation was as a delivery driver for a local company. He lives just outside Crossmaglen.

TEDDY COLLIGAN joined the retained service in Castlereagh in 1961. At the time his full-time employment was in the manufacturing industry. He retired in 1988. Following retirement from his main occupation, he and his wife Phoebe became guides at the Ulster Tower at the Thiepval Memorial in France for fifteen years. Teddy has a lifelong interest in motocross and continues to follow the sport.

AUBREY CRAWFORD joined the full-time service in 1974. He spent all of his service in Derry/Londonderry, moving from Northland Road station to Crescent Link as a fire safety officer, before retiring in 2002. Aubrey was regional treasurer of the Fire Brigades Union from 1976 until his retirement. He has been interested in music since he was a teenager and is president of the Hamilton Flute Band. Aubrey and his wife live in the city.

JIM CROZIER joined the retained service in Lurgan in 1969 and retired at the rank of sub officer in 2006. As his full-time occupation Jim worked in the clothing trade as a manager in a local shirt factory. Jim was awarded the MBE in 1999 for services to the Northern Ireland Fire Brigade. A keen wildlife photographer, Jim lives in Lurgan.

GORDON CUDDY joined the retained service in Dungannon in 1978 and retired as a Crew Commander in 2019. Gordon lives and works in the town – for many years, his family have had a clothes shop and he has worked there since he was a teenager.

STEVIE CUNNINGHAM joined the retained service in Antrim 1975 while working for the airport fire service at Aldergrove (now Belfast International). He subsequently entered the full-time service in 1977. He spent his entire full-time career in Belfast and retired at the rank of leading firefighter in 2003. Since his retirement, he and his wife Marian have discovered the joys of travel. They live in Belfast.

JAMES FITZPATRICK joined the auxiliary fire service in1953 and the retained service in 1961 He served in Newry and retired in 1981. His full-time employment was with the local education authority; in later years he was a security officer. James lives in Warrenpoint.

FRANCIE GILLEECE joined the retained service in Enniskillen in 1972 retiring as sub officer in 1998. As his full-time occupation Francie worked for the local council and was for many years the local licensing officer. He lives in Enniskillen.

BILLY HAMILTON joined the full-time service in Derry/ Londonderry in 1969. Initially serving at Northland Road in the city, he was promoted through the ranks and was based at various locations in the west of the province during his career. He retired at the rank of divisional officer in 2000. A lifelong sports enthusiast, Billy was a keen squash player and represented the NIFB at national competitions. Billy lives in the city.

WALTER JOHNSTON joined the full-time service in 1974, serving in Belfast. Subsequent promotions took him to Omagh and Portadown, from where he retired in 2007. Walter was involved for many years (both during his service and following retirement) in the International Road Rescue Competition, travelling around the world as both an event manager and judge. He was responsible for bringing the UK national competition to Northern Ireland for the first time in 2000. Walter is a keen sailor and regularly crews on local yachts on Lough Neagh and further afield. He lives in Magheralin.

HUGH KENNEDY joined the full-time service in 1965. He was based for most of his service in Northland Road fire station in Derry/Londonderry. He retired in 1996. Hugh had a long interest in horticulture and was closely involved in the city's participation in the Britain in Bloom TV series. Hugh passed away in 2019.

FRANK LOWRY joined the retained service in Castlereagh in 1962 and retired in 1988. When he joined the service, he worked full time in a local engineering company. In subsequent years he also worked as an MOD firefighter in Holywood. He lives in east Belfast.

HEATHER MAGOWAN joined the full-time service as a control operator in 1972. Initially based for training purposes in Belfast, she transferred to the control room at brigade headquarters in Lisburn shortly after, where she spent the remainder of her career. She retired at the rank of senior fire control operator in 2003. Heather has had a lifelong interest in animal welfare, 'fostering' more dogs than she cares to remember. She lives in Lisburn.

CHARLIE McAULEY joined the full-time service in 1978 and served the early part of his career in Belfast. He took up the post of station officer in Ballymoney in 1995 and was in charge of a number of retained stations in County Antrim. He returned to Belfast towards the end of his service and retired in 2012. Since retirement Charlie has worked in both a part-time and full-time capacity for a local mental health charity and as a guardian for vulnerable adults going through the justice system.

PAUL McCLELLAND joined the full-time service in 1979 and was posted to White Watch at Central Fire Station in Belfast where he spent all his service. He retired in 2001. He lives in south Belfast.

SAMMY McCULLOUGH joined the retained service in Bangor in 1968 and retired in 1989 as a result of an injury sustained on duty at a fire at the Queen's Court Hotel in 1987. Sammy's full-time occupation was as a maintenance engineer for the local council. A keen follower of sport, he lives in Bangor.

PADDY McGOWAN joined the retained service in Omagh in 1966. He was promoted to sub officer in 1972. He retired in 1991. His full-time employment was as a bus driver with Translink and he was promoted to district manager in 1989. He was the Omagh depot manager at the time of the Omagh bomb. He was active in local politics and an Independent local councillor on Omagh council for thirty-three years. In 2016, he was appointed High Sherriff of Tyrone in 2016. He was awarded the MBE in 1991. He and his wife live in Omagh.

JOE McKEE trained as a teacher and joined the retained service in Carrickfergus in 1973. He subsequently joined the full-time service in 1974 before returning to teaching following his graduation. He then rejoined the retained service (this time in Armagh) in 1978. He retired from the service in 1987. In 2011 he became chair of the Fire Authority, holding that office until 2015. Joe has always had music at the heart of his professional life, becoming the principal of the Belfast School of Music in 2002 and retiring in 2010. In 2006 he was awarded the OBE for services to music. Joe lives in the Sandown area of east Belfast.

GERARD McKENNA joined the retained service in Armagh in 1980 and retired as a leading fireman in 2009. His full-time occupation was as a vehicle mechanic in a local garage in Armagh. Since retirement he and his wife Bridie have travelled widely and continue to do so when grandchild-minding allows. They live in Armagh.

DESY MOYNES joined the retained service in Armagh in 1976 and then went into the full-time service in 1977. He spent a significant proportion of his early service in Central Fire Station in Belfast before being promoted into various posts, finishing his service as assistant district commander in Portadown. He retired in 2004. Desy's interests include fishing, shooting and 4X4s. He lives in Armagh city.

DERRICK MURRAY joined the retained service in Bangor in 1952 and retired at the rank of leading firefighter in 1986. During his full-time career he worked as a maintenance engineer for a number of local businesses. He and his wife Jean live in Greyabbey.

JOE O'LOUGHLIN joined the retained service in 1975 and was promoted to sub officer in 1982. His full-time occupation was as the owner/proprietor of a petrol station/garage on the main street of Belleek. He retired from the service in 1986. Joe is a keen and active local historian and has a particular interest in Fermanagh's role in the Second World War, particularly the coastal command seaplanes that were based on Lower Lough Erne. Joe lives just outside Belleek.

BOBBY POLLOCK joined the full-time service in 1966 having served in the British Army. He was based in a number of stations in Belfast and was the station commander of Central Station on Chichester Street when it was closed and relocated in 1992. Bobby was subsequently promoted to divisional officer with responsibility for staff welfare at service headquarters in Lisburn. He retired in 1998. Bobby has retained an interest both in fire service history and military history, especially in the First World War, and has travelled to the Western Front sites many times.

LIAM QUINN joined the retained service in Keady in 1976 and retired in 1996. In his full-time occupation, Liam worked for a number of years for a local bakery before taking up a post in a bakery in Armagh. Liam lives close to the fire station in Keady.

KEN RAMSEY joined the retained service in Enniskillen in 1976. He retired as a leading fireman in 2002. Ken's full-time occupation is as a picture framer and art supplies retailer in Enniskillen, where he and his wife Ann, a ceramicist, live.

DICKIE SEFTON joined the full-time service in 1955. He served in Belfast for all his career and retired at the rank of station officer in 1981. The injuries sustained when he was attacked with a petrol bomb in 1969 remain a legacy for him today. Dickie has a lifelong interest in cars and mechanical engineering. He and his wife live in the Stormont area of east Belfast.

HEATHER SMART joined the full-time service in 1991, becoming Northern Ireland's first female firefighter. She spent all her service at Knock Fire Station in east Belfast. Heather retired in 2018 and was awarded the MBE for her services to the advancement of women in the fire service.

JUNE SMITH joined the control room in 1972, serving initially in both Belfast and Lisburn before becoming permanently based in Lisburn following the consolidation of the control rooms within Northern Ireland in 1974. She retired in 1996 at the rank of senior fire control operator. June lives in Moira and continues to enjoy playing badminton.

GERRY STAFFORD joined the full-time service as a control operator in 1974. She was based for all her service in the control room at brigade headquarters in Lisburn. She retired at the rank of senior fire control operator in 1990. She lives in Lisburn.

COLIN TAGGART joined the full-time service in 1984 and was posted to Central Fire Station in Belfast. In 1989 he took advantage of a Fire Brigades Union scholarship scheme to go to Ruskin College, Oxford, and subsequently decided to leave the service to pursue further academic interests. Colin became interested in publishing and currently runs his own business in Wagga Wagga, New South Wales, where he has also become actively involved in local politics and commerce. He lives in Wagga Wagga with his Australian wife Stephanie.

Glossary

7/7
A code used by the fire service for bombs to make it less clear to anyone eavesdropping on their radio transmissions what they were dealing with. Used both when mobilising the crews and by OICs sending radio messages from the incident to the control room. A 'suspect 7/7' could turn out to be a real one and a '7/7' could turn out to be a hoax – an 'actuated 77' was a bomb that had detonated.

aerial
A generic term for any high-reach appliance. *See also* **turntable ladder** *and* **hydraulic platform**.

all persons accounted for
If people had been reported as missing or trapped at an incident, this is the message that the officer in charge relays to the control room to report that everyone is accounted for. *See also* **persons reported**.

ammunition technical officer (ATO)
An army officer involved in all aspects of the use of ammunition including bomb disposal, explosives accident investigation, storage, inspection and repair.

appliance
See **truck**.

branch
The nozzle on the end of a hose running from the pump. There were different types of branch: the largest were 'open-ended' while others – called 'hand-controlled' – could be turned on or off. *See also* **jet**.

breathing apparatus (BA)
Self-contained breathing apparatus that allowed firefighters
to enter smoke-filled areas, or areas where hazardous
chemicals were present. Every standard appliance had four
BA on board along with ancillary equipment.

call
A fire or other emergency incident that the service is called
to. This usually comes via the 999 system but can also
come from police or ambulance services. Also known as a
'shout', 'turn out', 'run' or 'fire call'.

Central
Central Fire Station on Belfast's Chichester Street was
originally the headquarters of the Belfast Fire Brigade. It
was built in the 1890s and has since been demolished. Also
known as 'Chi' or 'Chichester Street'.

control room
Where the 999 calls for the service are received. From here,
appliances are mobilised and radio communications with
them maintained. Since the early 1970s, the control room
has been located at service HQ in Lisburn. Also known as
'controls', 'control' and 'fire control'.

direct line
See **private wire.**

emergency tender (ET)
This appliance carried a considerable amount of extra
rescue equipment compared to a standard appliance,
including kit that was too big to be carried on a standard
truck. It also carried equipment for hazardous material
incidents and additional first aid kit.

engine room
Where the fire engines are normally parked in the fire station, ready to respond. Also known as the appliance bay.

escape
Another word for ladder. There were different types carried on the appliances.

fire call
See **call**.

fire car
Officers mobilised to incidents, who are not part of the crew on the fire engine, drive to the call in a car provided by the service. These vehicles have changed over the years but during most of the Troubles they were white and unmarked, except for some signage on the roof light. They have sirens and a fire service radio.

foam tender
An appliance that could make significantly more firefighting foam than a standard appliance. There is a very limited number of these in the service and they are used only in more serious incidents.

hose reel
A hose reel was a lighter weight hose intended for a quick attack on a small fire. It was rolled off a drum on the appliance and could immediately be put into operation. Although never designed for tackling serious or larger fires, the hose reel was often used when it was clear that getting a good water supply would be difficult and getting some water on the fire was better than none.

hydraulic platform
A 100ft/30m high reach mobile appliance that is articulated and has a working platform at the top.

jet
A line of hose running from a pump that had a nozzle (or 'branch') on the end.

L4P
A specially designed fire engine based on a Land Rover chassis intended for rural areas. It carries a limited amount of water and equipment but has some off-road capabilities. Often referred to as simply the Land Rover.

leading firefighter
The leading firefighter was the first rank and was generally in charge of a crew.

light portable pump (LPP)
A portable pump that can draw water from lakes and rivers. Carried on most standard fire appliances, it needs a minimum of four persons to lift it to wherever is needed.

officer in charge (OIC)
The senior person in charge of an incident. Depending on the severity, this could be any rank up to and including the chief fire officer. The term is often used to indicate the appliance commander – but also regularly refers to the overall commander at the fire or emergency.

persons reported
When a 999 caller indicates that people are missing or trapped, at imminent danger of being lost, the control room passes that information to the attending crews by the message 'persons reported'.

private wire
A direct telephone connection between police and fire
service control rooms that made for quick communications.

pump
See **truck**.

run
See **call**.

set
See **breathing apparatus**.

shift
See **watch**.

staff car
See **fire car**.

sub officer
In the retained service the sub officer (also known as the
'sub' and previously known as the section leader) was the
most senior rank – further ranks applied only to full-time
staff.

truck
Standard fire engine with a large built-in pump, hose,
ladders and rescue equipment.

turn out
See **call**.

turntable ladder
A large mobile extending ladder with 100ft/30m reach, used
for firefighting and rescues. Also known as 'TL' or 'TTL'.

watch
In full-time stations the 24hr/365 cover is maintained by four watches: Red, White, Blue and Green. From the late 1960s until the late 1970s, there were only three watches. Some retained stations also organised themselves into informal watches to help them manage their time off.

wheeled escape
A wooden ladder on wheels that was replaced towards the end of the 1970s.

Acknowledgements

Thanks to Helen Wright for her encouragement, support and superb professional skill. Also to Davy Kilpatrick for all the 'above and beyond' help so generously given. Thanks too to the following people who, in many different ways, helped and encouraged me – Roy Coulter, Gabriel Ferguson, Alan Harper, Graham Lowry, David Nichol, Ron Watson and Bill Wilsdon

Thanks to my wife Valerie for putting up with what so easily became a bit of an obsession.

And, of course, I am enormously grateful to all the contributors who shared their stories with such honesty and humanity – you have done us proud.